TO ACT IS TO DO

TO ACT IS TO DO

TO ACT IS TO DO

SIX CLASSES FOR TEACHERS AND ACTORS
BASED ON THE UTA HAGEN TECHNIQUE

RICHARD ALAN NICHOLS

39 WEST
PRESS

39 WEST PRESS
Kansas City, MO
www.39WestPress.com

39 WEST
Ⓟ Ⓡ Ⓔ Ⓢ Ⓢ

First Edition: January 2018

ISBN: 978-1-946358-06-6

Library of Congress Control Number: 2017960410

10 9 8 7 6 5 4 3 2 1

Book Design: j.d.tulloch
Proofreads: Mary Pinizzotto, Nancy Marcy, Atif Rome, Kathleen Warfel, Joey Kenig
Edits: Mark Gardiner, j.d.tulloch

39WP-25

To my mother:
for her love and encouragement.

❧

To my mentors:
Uta Hagen and the HB Studio.

CONTENTS

If you want a bourgeois existence, you shouldn't be an actor. You're in the wrong profession.

–Uta Hagen

FOREWORD

∾

THE MAGIC BEYOND
THE SCREEN DOOR

R ICHARD ALAN NICHOLS WAS born in 1934 to Alan and Ruth Nichols on a farm in Kensington, Connecticut. He lived there for the first eleven years of his life, until his father suddenly died at the age of thirty-five. His mother then sold the farm and purchased a beautiful, old house in Meriden, Connecticut.

During the summer of this emotionally difficult year for the Nichols family, Richard's mother rented a beach cottage on Long Island Sound in Westbrook, Connecticut. One weekend, his favorite aunt, Gertrude, came for a visit and took Richard to a local movie theatre.

While driving through Clinton, Connecticut on the way back to the beach cottage, Richard noticed a parking lot full of cars next to a building. He asked his aunt what was going on there. She told him that it was a summer theatre and people were there to watch a play. "Do you want to go in and see what it is all about?" she asked.

He excitedly replied, "Oh yes, can we?!"

Aunt Gertrude parked the car and then led Richard to the side of the building. They walked up a flight of concrete steps, sat down on the top step, and watched the rest of the first act through the screen door. Even though he could only see three-quarters of the stage, Richard was riveted by the story and what he saw on stage.

Richard empathized with the victim in the drama. He had never seen anything with this kind of magic: wonderful actors, lights, costumes, sets, and an audience captivated by the plight of a frightened wife being manipulated by her husband.

When the first act ended, Aunt Gertrude asked Richard if he wanted to see the rest of the performance. "Oh yes!" Richard replied. "This is so much better than the movies!"

They entered the lobby of the Clinton Playhouse and stood on the marble floor, staring at the well-dressed audience members who were smoking cigarettes. When the lights in the lobby flickered, the people put out their cigarettes in the sand containers and entered the theatre. Gertrude and Richard decided to "second act" the play—the process of waiting for intermission, entering the lobby with the paying audience, finding empty seats, and watching the rest of the performance without paying—and were the last to enter. As the house lights faded, they found two seats in the back of the orchestra and enjoyed the rest of the performance.

The play was *Angel Street* by Patrick Hamilton and starred Francis Lederer, a Czech actor who starred in silent films before playing major supporting roles in Hollywood films of the 30s, 40s, and 50s. In 1944 *Angel Street* was adapted into the film *Gaslight*, starring Ingrid Bergman and Charles Boyer.

That night Richard relived images of the play and could not sleep. He now knew how he would spend the rest of his life.

Richard soon appeared in all the school plays. Each summer, during Aunt Gertrude's visits, the two spent afternoons on the beach; in the evenings she took him to various straw hat theatres. When Richard was a teenager, he took the train, by himself, either to New Haven or Hartford to see tours of successful plays or plays that were being previewed prior to their New York openings.

For Richard, the theatre was a magic place, and the magic started the minute he walked into the lobby on his way buy a ticket from the box office: in the air were the smell of excitement and the wonder of expectation. As he waited for the house to open, Richard's adrenalin started to pump. He watched other audience members arrive and wondered if they were experiencing the same emotions that he felt.

Once inside the theatre and seated in the second balcony, he first studied the architecture and then fixated on the curtain, wondering what would be revealed. The excitement was almost unbearable. When the curtain rose (or parted) and the actors appeared on stage, transforming themselves into the characters they embodied, Richard realized that they possessed the real magic, that the actors were the true magicians of theatre.

At the age of sixteen, Richard talked a friend into driving him to New Haven where a production of George Bernard Shaw's *St. Joan* was previewing at the Shubert Theatre before its New York premiere. The star of the play was Uta Hagen. He didn't understand all the philosophical arguments in the play but was captivated by the performance of Ms. Hagen. The price of a second balcony ticket, where he always sat, was $1.80, a far cry from the single ticket price of $845 for *Hamilton* on Broadway.

In 1957 Richard moved to New York and auditioned for Uta Hagen's acting class the following year. He was accepted. In 1967 he worked with the Obie winning Second Story Players. The company was commissioned to work on a project in St. Louis involving performance and teaching. He moved to St. Louis, where he stayed until 1978. Finally, he moved to Kansas City, where he currently resides.

Richard has worked as an actor or director for all of the major theatres in Kansas City. In 1985 he founded The Actor's Craft Studio, where he continues to teach acting.

Richard's story is not that unusual. But what makes his story unique is the fact that he has stuck with his dream since 1946 after seeing that production of *Angel Street* through a screen door. Little did the actors of that play realize the impact their work would have on an eleven-year-old boy who, with Aunt Gertrude leading the way, second acted their performance.

TO ACT IS TO DO

MY LIFE IN PURSUIT OF BECOMING A PLAYER

THEATRE IS MY PASSION, but acting did not come easy for me. I dreamed of becoming a great actor and pursued it as though it were an obsession. I wanted success too much, and the idea of failure terrified me. Always striving for perfection, I never believed I was good enough and felt self-conscious knowing how badly I was acting. My body would become saturated with tension, my stomach twisted in hard knots, and my mouth devoid of moisture. I was a basket case.

Each time I stepped on stage, it seemed that I was rewarded by that old demon: failure. A friend once asked me an important question: "If acting is so painful for you, then why do you do it?" I replied, "I don't know. I just have to." So, I continued to work hard, trying to get it right. I didn't realize it then, but during all those failures I was sowing healthy seeds that I would later harvest in my work.

Throughout my life in pursuit of becoming a player, I have given some good performances and some other performances that were not so good. But I have never given up on my dream. I have spent my life perfecting the craft of acting, turning that craft into art, and passing that craft on to my students in hope that they, too, would create art.

In this book I have attempted to put into written form the work in which I have been involved as a teacher since the late 1960s. Based on the mistakes I made and the problems I had while learning my craft, I have tried to make the structure as clear as possible for both teachers and actors. There is purposeful repetition in the writing.

While developing my craft as an actor, I was a slow learner, and repetition was necessary. I needed to hear, over and over again, the acting structures and lessons (and how to work with them).

First, I would understand intellectually the acting concepts, and then, much later, after constant repetition, the "light bulb" would come on. Eventually, I was able to execute the concepts in my work, which I have seen happen in my students' work as well. I love the theatre.

‹ BOSTON ›

IT WAS 1953, MY first year at Boston University. I was eighteen years old and had been cast in two plays: as one of the players in *Hamlet* and as Reverend Harper in *Arsenic and Old Lace* by Joseph Kesselring. In both plays I was a nervous wreck and a disaster.

The university had just purchased the abandoned Esquire Theatre on Huntington Avenue, a former art film house. It was located across the street from Symphony Hall, home of the Boston Symphony. Down the street on the corner sat the New England Conservatory of Music and farther west the Boston Museum of Fine Arts and the Old Boston Opera House. Huntington Avenue was called "The Avenue of the Arts." Having been born on a farm in rural Connecticut, this world was new for me.

The theatre was originally designed by J. Williams Beal and Sons as a legitimate theatre, which had a history in the community. It opened, with 941 seats, in 1925 as the Repertory Theatre of Boston.

This venue was to become the home for classes and performances for Boston University's Theatre and Opera Department. The theatre was cavernous and reminded me of Konstantin Stanislavski's words in his book *An Actor Prepares*: "I had hardly stepped on to the stage when there loomed up in front of me the immense hole of the proscenium arch, and beyond it an endless expanse of dark mist."

I remember the disaster of playing the Reverend Harper in

Arsenic and Old Lace. I was on stage at the opening of the play, drinking tea with the two old ladies. The rattle of my tea cup in the saucer could be heard in the last row of the balcony. I can still hear it echo. I was sure that I was a failure, but quitting wasn't an option.

The next year, the theatre department changed. The faculty was replaced by professional teachers, directors, dancers, and designers from New York. The department also included an opera component headed by Sarah Caldwell, the renowned director and conductor.

I remember the first day of classes that September morning and being the first student standing on the steps of the theatre waiting for the doors to be unlocked. I was excited, nervous, and eager.

The university had given scholarships to a number of students who had graduated from The High School of Performing Arts in New York. They arrived in Boston with an attitude of experience, confidence, and worldly sophistication.

They also wore a lot of black. The girls wore black eye liner. One young man walked around with a cat on his shoulder. I was intimidated. Were all of these things the prerequisites for being a good actor? And there was one more problem to deal with: I was hiding in the deepest, darkest part of the closet.

One night, a group of us were at The Lobster Claw, a watering hole adjacent to the theatre, when we received a phone call from one of the young women who dressed in black and wore black eye liner. She threatened to jump off the Charles River Bridge unless someone would come and talk to her. No one went, and she didn't jump. We were all so young and dramatic.

My acting teacher, Alexander Kirkland, was a nice man. He had been an actor in New York and Hollywood, mostly in the 1930s. He told great stories about his experiences and the stars with whom he had worked. For a time, he was married to Gypsy Rose Lee. He also explained the proper location of one's waist, believing that most of the men in the class were belting their trousers too low.

He talked about *objectives* and *actions*. He told us that actors must know what their character wants (*the objective*) and what they must do to achieve that *objective* (*the action*). This information was new to me. I understood it intellectually but didn't know what to do with it.

His evaluations of our work were usually judgmental rather than constructive. He'd say, "It's not believable. You have no understanding of character. Your voice and body needs work, and you have to get free with your emotions."

In the 1950s, acting was all about emotion. "The Method," Stanislavsky, and The Actor's Studio were paramount. Our heroes were Marlon Brando and James Dean. Anyone in class who could cry and produce real water was praised by the teacher. We were told, "That's what good acting is all about." Everyone worked hard to produce the big emotions.

I remember I had—and still can't believe I did this—the guts to request an audition for The Actor's Studio in New York. Much to my surprise and trepidation, the studio responded with a time and date. I found a scene partner who was more than willing to work with me. We chose a scene from *Mourning Becomes Electra* by Eugene O'Neill. During rehearsals, we worked our tails off in an attempt to impress the studio with our "free emotions."

Having little money, we took the milk train from Boston to New York, which left Boston at midnight and arrived in New York at seven in the morning. Our audition wasn't until eight that evening. So, we hung around the city, drinking coffee and running lines every twenty minutes.

At seven o'clock, we arrived at the hallowed studio at 432 West 44th Street in Hell's Kitchen. The brick building looked like an old church. We entered a small, makeshift green room and were met by a male receptionist who told us to take a seat. For over an hour we waited there, sitting on uncomfortable wooden chairs and watching other actors come and go.

When our turn to audition arrived, our names were called, and we walked up a flight of stairs into a dark room, which was lighted only at one end. We entered the lighted area, introduced ourselves, and announced our scene selection. The people for whom we were auditioning couldn't be seen in the back of the dark hall. They thanked us for coming all the way from Boston. I don't remember how we made it through the audition, but we did. Then, all of a sudden, my partner burst into tears. This crying had never happened in our many rehearsals. I wondered, recalling what we had learned in class about crying ("That's what good acting is all about."), if the tears were calculated to impress. In actuality, the tears were probably the result of the extreme stress of the event. After the audition, we took another milk train back to Boston.

Several weeks later, I received a letter from The Actor's Studio, rejecting me. However, they suggested that I continue my studies at the university and audition for them again in the future.

At the university, Mr. Kirkland continued to lecture us on the importance of *objectives* and *actions*, but I still couldn't pin them down. I remember struggling to find a single *objective* for a scene from *The Seagull* by Anton Chekhov. Prior to rehearsal, I diligently wrote verbs (*actions*) in the margin of the text. The verbs I wrote down never seemed to work. They didn't seem to fit with what I was receiving from my partner. Besides, I didn't know how to play them. I was trying to do what I thought I was supposed to do. It was an intellectual puzzle, and I was never good at puzzles.

I don't mean to paint a bleak picture of Boston University. I learned many things there while working with and observing professional directors—José Quintero, Alan Schneider, Peter Cass, David Pressman, and Curt Conway—which was inspiring. I took a course in Modern Drama, taught by Elliot Norton, the esteemed Boston critic. I read the plays of Ibsen, Strindberg, Chekhov, Shaw, and many others. I also learned the all-important lesson of discipline in the theatre.

Peter Cass, a director and teacher from New York, had been hired by the university to direct *The Crucible* by Arthur Miller. There were several callback auditions. It was a Friday evening, and we were all in the green room waiting for the cast list to be posted. The stage manager came in and said, "Nichols? Mr. Cass wants to talk to you." I went down the hall to his office. Almost as if he was daring me, Mr. Cass asked, "I am thinking of you for Paris. Can you do it?" I replied, "Yes, sir."

Late one Friday evening, some of us went to "The Claw" for a beer. At this point, we had been in rehearsal for two weeks, and the call for the Saturday morning was ten o'clock. After a few drinks, I returned to my apartment and fell asleep. The next thing I knew, it was ten-thirty in the morning. I didn't have a phone. So, I dressed as fast as I could, ran five blocks to the theatre, and dashed up the stairs to the rehearsal hall. Mr. Cass was waiting for me, smoking a Viceroy cigarette with the filter clinched between his teeth. "You will come to rehearsal one hour early for the next week and report to the stage manager," he demanded. Since that day, I have never been late to a rehearsal.

The school was a mixture of undergraduate and graduate students in the same classes. During my third year, a woman a few years older than me enrolled as a graduate student.

She had been a registered physical therapist and was thrown into the theatre classes with little understanding of what was going on. I remember sitting with her on the steps of the theatre, where we discussed acting, smoked cigarettes, and watched life go by on Huntington Avenue. I tried to communicate what limited knowledge I had about the mystery and craft of acting. While talking to her, the mystery started to unravel for me.

We became great friends, soul mates, and started working together on scenes. I finally began to relax in my work. We were teaching and learning from each other and were rewarded with approval from our teachers and peers. Her name: Olympia Dukakis.

At the time, I was struggling with my sexuality. I knew I was homosexual, and in my mind, I thought that being gay would be the death for my career as an actor. It was the 1950s and American culture was much more homophobic than today.

I soon met Joanna, a graduate student in costume design, at a party. She was older and had been married, which ended in divorce. We started dating and eventually living together. I thought this relationship would be a "cure." It wasn't.

‹ NEW YORK ›

AFTER FINISHING OUR WORK at Boston University, Joanna and I moved to New York and soon discovered that she was pregnant. We married, and our son Peter was born on April 29, 1958.

Later that year, I auditioned for Uta Hagen's acting class at the

HB Studio. I was accepted and awarded a scholarship. I couldn't believe it. For me, this was the pinnacle of success. It was an exciting time for young actors in New York. When they weren't working on a show, actors would go back to class. Bobby Lewis even taught a special night class for working actors that started at eleven o'clock. I will never forget my first scene in Ms. Hagen's class; it was from Ketti Frings' *Look Homeward, Angel*, adapted from the novel by Thomas Wolfe, who was my idol. I had read two of his novels: that one and *Of Time and the River*, from which I had even memorized a passage: "We were young and drunk and twenty, and could never die!"

I was assigned a scene partner, Sheila Coonan, to play my mother. Sheila had worked on Broadway, Off Broadway, in films, and on television. We rehearsed in her apartment, a cold water flat on Thompson Street in the Village. At class that Wednesday afternoon, we were the last scene presented. Ms. Hagen gave Sheila her notes and asked if I would stay for a minute after class. My heart started beating a mile a minute. I just knew she was going to tell me that she had made a mistake and I needed to be in a different class—or that I should consider another profession.

The class ended, and as the students were leaving, she came back to where I was sitting, pulled up a chair beside me, and said, "Dick," she called me Dick, "you don't have to work so hard. It's there." After that, I can't remember her exact words, but the essence was something like this:

> Dick, you were forcing the emotion. You don't want to do that. You don't need to do that. Don't even think about emotion. Let it happen the way it wants to. Let the emotion take you. And once it does, you need to fight for normalcy. That's what we do in real life. For next week, just focus on *place*: the backyard of your mother's boarding house. Remember, you have lived here all your life. You know it like the back of your hand. I will see you next week.

I immediately thought of the backyard on the farm where I was born and breathed a sigh of relief. And when next week came, the scene was better.

I continued to work hard and eventually performed in several projects at the studio. Gradually, I earned some work Off Broadway and Off Off Broadway. I studied with Ms. Hagen for five years, and the HB Studio became an important part of my life and life's work.

Founded in 1945 by Herbert Berghof, who had been a successful actor and director in his native Vienna, Austria before fleeing the Nazis and arriving in America in 1939, the HB Studio opened in rented space at the Charles Weidman Dance Studio on 16th Street.

Also in 1945, Berghof was hired as a replacement actor in the play *The Whole World Over*, which was directed by Harold Clurman and starred Uta Hagen, who Berghof convinced to teach at the studio. They were married ten years later.

In 1950 the studio moved to a three-story loft in Chelsea, and in 1958 another move occurred: to an old stable they purchased at 120 Bank Street in the West Village. The studio now occupies the two adjoining buildings.

The fee to study at the studio was affordable for the time: $8 per class. And the studio's mission was to create an environment where actors, directors, and playwrights could study, experiment, share ideas, collaborate, and, hopefully, contribute to improve the state of the theatre.

In 1962 the students at HB were given free tickets to the first preview of Edward Albee's *Who's Afraid of Virginia Woolf?*, staring Uta Hagen. I went to that performance and also to the opening night performance on October 13, 1962, which I paid for. I had never been to an opening night on Broadway. Both performances were wonderful. The opening night performance received more laughs. Ms. Hagen was amazing. Her total being embodied her character, Martha, and she won the 1962 Tony Award for best actress.

Ms. Hagen, however, was not the first choice for Martha by producers Richard Barr and Clinton Wilder, director Alan Schneider, and playwright Edward Albee. Their first choice was Geraldine Page, Ms. Hagen's former student. When Page demanded that they hire her current teacher, Lee Strasberg, as her coach during rehearsals, the producers, director, and playwright felt that this would be problematic and decided, instead, to ask Ms. Hagen.

She accepted the role, and the rest is history.

Nearly forty years later, on Sunday, November 14, 1999, Uta Hagen (at the age of eighty), Jonathan Price, Mia Farrow, and Mathew Broderick performed a one night only stage reading of *Who's Afraid of Virginia Woolf?* at the Majestic Theatre on Broadway as a fund raiser for The Playwrights Foundation at the HB Studio. Two weeks later, Vincent Canby, in the *New York Times*, wrote:

> For most of us time is inflexible and cruel, a wearing out of resources, a diminishment of powers. But when time bends, as the title of Arthur Miller's memoir suggests, it can, among other things, accommodate, deepen and make possible the sort of one-of-a-kind performance of which theatrical legends are made. Ms. Hagen's great, bawdy one-night stand with the role of Martha now becomes one of those legends, her physical and psychological presence possibly even enriched by everything that has happened since the first time she played the role ... Only memory keeps the living theatre alive, recalling the particular circumstances in which time wasn't stopped but, instead, its passage celebrated. It is only in an acute awareness of the finite, during a performance you know will never be exactly duplicated, that you glimpse the meaning of the infinite.

At Ms. Hagen's memorial service, Edward Albee said that Uta Hagen was a better Martha at eighty than she was at forty-three, if that is at all possible.

I was so fortunate to have spent five years in the environment at HB. I not only studied with one of the great masters of acting, but I also studied speech, vocal production, and dance. I had the opportunity to work with some wonderful people, and I can't thank the studio enough. What I learned from my mentors, I am now attempting to pass on to my students.

Herbert Berghof and Uta Hagen, together, were a mighty force in the education and inspiration of many theatre artists in the twentieth century. They are gone now, but their work continues to influence artists in the twenty-first century. At 120-124 Bank Street, their work lives on.

The list of students who have studied at the HB Studio is mind boggling. In the beginning there were Mildred Donnock, Betty Field, Lee Grant, Mira Rostova, Eli Wallach, Jo Van Fleet, Hal Holbrook, Harvey Korman, Jack Lemmon, E.G. Marshall, Steve McQueen, Anne Meara, Geraldine Page, Charles Nelson Reilly, Jason Robards, Eva Marie Saint, George Segal, Maureen Stapleton, Jerry Stiller, Fritz Weaver, and Gene Wilder.

Later, students included F. Murray Abraham, Anne Bancroft, Candice Bergen, Jeff Bridges, Mathew Broderick, Jill Clayburgh, Stockard Channing, Billy Crystal, Hope Davis, Sandy Dennis, Robert De Niro, Faye Dunaway, Rita Gardner, Whoopi Goldberg, Harvey Keitel, Jessica Lang, Marsha Mason, Bette Midler, Liza Minnelli, Cynthia Nixon, Al Pacino, Sarah Jessica Parker, Amanda Peet, Christopher Reeve, Kyra Sedgewick, Jon Stewart, Barbra Streisand, Lily Tomlin, Sigourney Weaver, and many, many others, myself included.

‹ St. Louis ›

In 1967 I moved from New York to St. Louis after accepting a job, part of a federally funded project called Metropolitan Educational Center in the Arts (MECA), which contained a theatre component: a company of actors were to create and perform theatre pieces in the schools of the greater St. Louis area. Also, I was to instruct teachers in theatre techniques, with the hope that they would use these techniques as teaching tools for different subjects.

To guide me in this work, I was provided a copy of Viola Spolin's book, *Improvisation for the Theatre*. The book, a compilation of theatre games originally designed for children at Chicago's Hull House, later became an important text in the founding of Second City, the famous improvisational theatre in Chicago.

Joanna, my wife, and I worked together in the teaching aspect of this program. We also taught students in separate workshops. Our classes were improvisational. For example, I would explain an acting problem—such as *place, relationship, objective*, etc.—and Joanna would talk to the actors privately, setting up an improvised scene scenario with *objectives* for them to explore within the designated acting problem. I would then evaluate the work.

A great deal of the work took place in inner city schools. Racial tensions were high following the assassinations of John F. Kennedy and Medgar Evers in 1963, Malcom X in 1965, and Martin Luther King Jr. and Robert F. Kennedy in 1968.

Joanna and I decided to create a company of actors, which grew out of our workshops. The company included Liz Carpenter, Ray Collins, Pat Williams, Val Williams, Ricky Curtis, John Cothrane, and Ed Brown. Jazz musicians Julius Hemphill and J.D. Parren appeared as guest performers. Each talented artist brought to the performance, which included music and comedy, rich stories of African American culture and tales of persecution.

Joanna and I were also teaching at Washington University, and we incorporated some of our students into the company, which received small grants as a result of its diversity. The city hired us to conduct workshops and performances at inner city community centers, an additional resource for aspiring black actors.

Another member of the company was our son, Peter, who at fourteen years old was the company's youngest member. He had a real gift for comedy and did many, wonderful voices. People would ask, "Is Peter performing tonight?" He had an appetite for performance and built up quite a following. Years later, Peter went into radio and now hosts the morning show on Connecticut's i-98.3. For over thirty years his voices, quick wit, and political savvy have endeared him to many listeners.

As the theatre company grew, we were also hired by the Black Artists Group (BAG). Malinké Robert Elliott (then Malinké Kenyatta), BAG's executive director, was a friend, and he hired us to conduct a series of classes on Monday nights. The group was composed of musicians, poets, writers, dancers, and actors. It was exciting, and we looked forward to those sessions. The work was improvisational, and the students had an uninhibited sense of joy in their work. Their energy, commitment, and passion to create inspired us.

Eventually, the board of directors of BAG fired us, as they felt their money should go directly to someone in the black community. While this hurt, we understood their position. Moving on ...

Every Saturday, our company performed free improvised events, with much of our work dealing with political satire, racial issues, the Vietnam War, and audience interaction. Tensions ran high during this period of American history. For example, Joel Achtenberg, one of our students, was part of the group of war protesters that stormed and torched the Washington University ROTC building on May 6, 1970 in response to the killing of four Kent State student-activists by the Ohio National Guard. Thousands cheered as the building burned. In 1971 Joel was convicted of violating a federal anti-sabotage law and sentenced to fifteen years in prison. The Eighth Circuit Court of Appeals overturned the conviction and granted him a new trial. He was acquitted in 1973 at the age of twenty-six.

These events, and more, seeped into our work, which included street theatre and performances at political demonstrations and community events, with Joanna setting up the premises for related improvised scenes. The name of our company: Saturday Nite Leftovers.

One of the key members of the Saturday Nite Leftovers was Washington University student Joey Kenig, an excellent actor and musician. In 2015 I reconnected with him in St. Louis. Now retired from a successful career as a builder and furniture maker, he is currently pursuing another passion: writing music and performing. He has released two brilliant CDs of original songs and world music.

Actors from that company who have continued working in the performing arts include Lynn & Ron Cohen, actors in regional and dinner theatre and, more recently, major feature films, television, and the recent Off Broadway play *Traveling Lady*; Julius Hemphill, founder of the World Saxophone Quartet; J.D. Parren, jazz director at The Harlem School of the Arts (he has performed with Stevie Wonder and John Lennon); Denny Krausnick, director of training at Shakespeare & Company; Sturgis Warner, actor-director living in New York and working Off and Off Off Broadway; John Cothrane, actor in regional theatre and feature films; and Mark Edelman, presenter and producer of touring Broadway productions. In 1989, Mark hired me to play John Honeyman in Lee Blessing's thought provoking and funny two-character play *A Walk in the Woods*.

Other actors who worked with us at different times during the company's five-year-run include: Jeff Hammers, Stuart Goodale, Hayes Harrison, Karla Goodman, Christie Simmons, Kevin Coleman, Mike Ferry, Carol Lowenstein, Deb Orland, Volker VonGlassenapp, Robert Miller, Renee Forgash, Carla Bromberg, Amy Ernlund, Bill LaBath, and Else Schmidt and Joy Fisher, both supporters and fundraisers for our work. All apologies to anyone I have forgotten to mention.

‹ KANSAS CITY ›

IN 1973 THE AMERICAN Psychiatric Association voted to remove homosexuality from its list of mental disorders. For me, this decision was liberating. Finally, I realized that I was neither sick nor a pervert. Hiding my true sexual orientation had been detrimental for me as an actor. I couldn't be myself and had to pretend I was someone else.

Joanna had been very helpful in working with me as a teacher and co-director of the company, but myriad problems existed in our marriage. I was living a lie and needed to accept my true sexuality. In 1978 we agreed to divorce.

At this point of my life, I really wanted to do something different. After ten years of working with improvisation, I was burned out. I missed the work process of traditional theatre. I wanted to follow my training and work on plays and teach scene study. I was forty-four years old, and it was now or never.

A friend encouraged me to audition for Missouri Repertory Theatre in Kansas City (now the KC Rep). I got the job and moved to Kansas City, where I have taught at Park University, Avila University, Rockhurst University, the Unicorn Theatre, and New Directions Theatre.

In 1980 I met visual artist and set-costume designer Atif Rome, who became my lover, teacher, best friend, and life partner. We have been together for over thirty years and have enjoyed working as a team on many productions.

I decided, in 1985, that it was time to start teaching private classes. Having previously worked with the Viola Spolin theatre games, I soon realized that the games could be reconstructed in a novel way to teach beginning actors the basic ingredients of the Uta Hagen technique. Thus, the Actor's-Craft Studio was born.

At first, classes were taught at the Westport Allen Center, which was home of the Kansas City Ballet. The space was great, but for each class, we had to carry our gear up three long flights of stairs to reach the studio.

Eventually, Atif and I rented an old, rambling three-story house on Warwick Boulevard in midtown Kansas City. We lived on the second floor, Atif's studio occupied the third floor, and the first floor became the new home of the Actor's-Craft Studio. Not only did I teach classes there, but the studio also became a place for performance, including two short pieces—*Connections* and *Incidents*—written by one of my students, Eric Adler, a journalist for the *Kansas City Star,* who writes in-depth stories about the human condition. The students loved working with him.

Other projects included *3 X* by Romulus Linney, *The Night Larry Kramer Kissed Me* by David Drake, and *Ti Jean Blues*, a compilation of the writings of Jack Kerouac, by JoAnne Akalaitis. We also presented two original plays that I wrote, *Land* and *Detours*, with all characters played by my students.

We worked out of the Warwick Boulevard space for eleven years, until one Saturday morning in the late spring of 1999 when the landlord interrupted class and informed me that he planned on moving back into the house. Atif and I soon found a small but wonderful house in South Hyde Park, which we purchased. It took over a year, but in August 2001 the converted basement became the new home of the Actor's-Craft Studio.

Unfortunately, the studio was not suitable for performance but has served as rehearsal space for new projects involving many of my students, including *Jesus on Toast* by Mark Gardiner, which debuted at the 2015 Kansas City Fringe Festival. The studio has also been used as rehearsal space for Actors' Equity Project Code readings of *Visiting Mr. Green* by Jeff Baron, *Painting Churches* by Tina Howe, and *Collected Stories* by Donald Margulies.

In 2008 I changed the structure of my classes. Up to that point, I had been teaching two separate classes: one for beginning students and another for more advanced students. I wondered what might happen if I combined classes and worked with each actor at their own specific level of development.

The results were impressive. In the combined class advanced students revisited the fundamental exercises, which brought new dimensions to their work. When beginning students observed the advanced students, they immediately saw where their work could go. By simply fine tuning the beginning-level exercises, veteran actors gained fresh insights into their craft. They discovered new and exciting choices as they solved basic acting problems, thereby gaining deeper understanding as actors and finding value in the exercises in a new way.

According to *Jesus on Toast* playwright and friend Mark Gardiner, the "craftsman, in perfecting their craft, will eventually turn the craft into a piece of art." Just as a dancer is always perfecting a plié and a musician is always reviewing basic scales, an actor, too, must have the discipline necessary to perfect their craft and create art.

◄ THE STRUGGLE ►

I HAVE NOTICED THAT after the Academy Awards there is an increase in enrollment in my classes. But very few actors live the life projected on red carpet interviews or in gossip columns.

With so many actors looking for work, few actually make it to "the big time." For actors who do find work, it is typically in print, commercials, minor television and film roles, and—if lucky—Off Broadway, dinner theatre, and regional theatre. Many good actors pursuing a full-time career in this business struggle to keep going, both emotionally and financially.

I learned this reality when I was studying at Boston University. For a time I lived in an apartment with three other theatre students. The rent was $75 a month. In today's world that sounds like a great deal. But to poor students—some of whom might have had part-time work as dishwashers—in the 1950s, this amount was a huge sum to come up with every month. With most of our time being spent in classes, rehearsals, and crew work for the up-coming production, finding time to work a paying job was difficult.

But somehow we always found a way to scrape together enough money to pay the rent. After breathing a sigh of relief, we hoped we would make enough money during the rest of the month to buy food and pay for other living expenses. By the time the first of the next month rolled around, we were broke and panic, once again, settled in.

Our landlady, Mrs. Cole, who lived on the first floor, would typically comply with our requests for a grace period. The apartment was on the top floor of an old, four-story brick walk-up in the Back Bay section of Boston. The hall outside of our apartment was filthy and smelled of something rotten. The heat in the building was turned off at ten o'clock in the evening. While trying to sleep, I could hear rats running across the roof and in-between the walls. At that time Boston was a city full of rats.

After moving to New York, I took a job with the now defunct Eastern Airlines, working from midnight to eight in the morning. I did this for ten years, which allowed me time to attend acting class, make the rounds to the offices of producers and agents, and rehearse and perform in the evenings.

At the offices of agents and producers, the receptionist, who was usually polite, would accept my head shot and resume. I am sure that as soon as I left the photo and resume went into the round file.

After about two years I was finally cast in a showcase production of *The Flowering Peach* by Clifford Odets at the Curt Conway Studio on West 48th Street. Actors were not paid. It was supposed to be an opportunity for agents to see our work. To the best of my knowledge, agents did not show up. But, at last, I finally had the chance to work.

Two years later, the director of *The Flowering Peach*, Isaiah "Sony" Shaffer, called and asked if I was interested in replacing Joe Chaikin in an Off Broadway production of Bertolt Brecht's one act play *The Exception and the Rule*. Joe was leaving the production to go on a European tour with The Living Theatre (an important avant-garde political theatre company of the 1960s through the 1980s).

At the time I had a bad cough and was spitting up a lot of yellow green stuff. But this was my big break and nothing was going to stand in my way. After the first rehearsal, Sony said to me, "You better see somebody about that cough." On my way home I went to the emergency room at Roosevelt Hospital, where I was diagnosed with double pneumonia and hospitalized for two months. Unfortunately, I lost out on that job.

A series of auditions followed, resulting in rejection after rejection, which took its toll on my spirit. I tried to start a theatre; it proved to be an artistic, financial, and emotional disaster. I felt I was going nowhere fast and started drinking a lot of cheap vodka. I had become discouraged by the commercial theatre community in New York and was ready to call it quits.

The airline was opening a new office in Seattle, Washington, and I put in a transfer. Two months later, it came through. But I had second thoughts about the transfer and withdrew it. I had started to work with a company of actors, The Second Story Players, in a store front on East Broadway in the Village, doing new plays Off-Off-Broadway. The space could only seat thirty-five audience members, but we were playing to capacity crowds. After the fire department shut us down for not having safe exits, we moved to a second floor loft on 23rd Street and 7th Avenue. At about this time, the opportunity to work in St. Louis presented itself.

My life was far from the fantasy theatre life that I had imagined. Today, the struggle continues. It is still a challenge to pay the bills and find work, the work to which I have dedicated my life.

Do I have regrets? There have been times that I have made bad choices, both personally and professionally. But I have no regrets about living my life as an actor and director and working in the theatre.

While at Boston University, Peter Cass told me, "Actors don't reach their potential until the age of fifty." I have found that statement to be true. For me, my best work occurred at age seventy-nine, when I played Nonno, the ninety-seven-year-old poet in *The Night of the Iguana* by Tennessee Williams. Throughout my career in the theatre, it has been those types of experiences that have fueled my journey in pursuit of becoming a player. Other actors will tell different stories: some more successful than others but all variations of *the struggle*.

NOTE TO TEACHERS: If any of your students want to pursue acting as a profession, you need to give them a realistic picture of what lies ahead, similar to what I have described.

NOTE TO ACTORS: If your goal is similar to mine: be advised of the struggle. It is not my intent to discourage you from following your dreams. I just want you to have a realistic approach to your work and expectations. For most of us, it is not an easy life. But if you have to do it, then do it.

‹ A FINAL THOUGHT ›

DURING MANY YEARS OF teaching, I have attempted to create, through a process of trial and error, improvised exercises designed to speak to all actors, regardless of experience. While some of these exercises may have been derivatives of the Spolin games, I tried to change their focus so that they related directly to the acting concepts I learned from Uta Hagen in both her classes and books.

Ms. Hagen only taught professional actors, and I have always welcomed actors of all skill levels. I would like to thank all of the students who have helped me refine these exercises over the last thirty years. Their input has been invaluable.

I am reminded of an experience I had while studying with Ms. Hagen. As part of my scholarship duties, I was required to monitor a lecture she gave to new students the first time she met with them. I don't remember the specific acting concept she presented that day, but during the lecture, I had one off those "Eureka!" moments. After class, I told Ms. Hagen how great her point was and that I had never heard her bring it up before. She replied, "I always include that in my lectures. You are just hearing it differently now. You are hearing it on a new level of understanding."

Since starting the Actor's-Craft Studio, I have encouraged my students to purchase Ms. Hagen's book, *A Challenge for the Actor*, which should be a constant reference for actors, as it has been for me. Ms. Hagen greatly influenced my work as an actor, teacher, and director.

I wrote this book, therefore, in hope that my words will serve as a guide for actors who, unfortunately, never had the opportunity to study with Ms. Hagen, who died in 2004, and for teachers to use in their secondary school, under-graduate, and graduate classes. I love the theatre.

CHAPTER 1

~

CLASS AND REHEARSAL PROCEDURES

AS CHILDREN, WE LEARNED to play and discovered imagination. We had enormous curiosity about the world in which we lived as we struggled to understand and communicate. We were amazed at the things we found out about ourselves and our immediate environment. As actors, we must hold on to that curiosity and imagination. It will serve us until the day we die.

I grew up on a farm, and at family gatherings, I wanted to stay in the living room with the adults and listen to them gossip. They encouraged me to go outside and play with the other children. When I refused, they went on with their stories, probably thinking, "He won't understand." The stories sparked my imagination as I visualized the people and events in them. For me, this was where the drama occurred, and it was more exciting than playing with a ball.

I believe our job as actors—our purpose and mission—is to reveal to the audience the human joys, dreams, expectations, pains, fears, insecurities, demons, and struggles of being alive. Theatre is all about the connection between actor and audience that happens live—in the right now. It is in the immediate present tense—where we are together as one—that we communicate.

If we, as actors, personally identify with the characters we are playing, then the audience possibly can gain insights into their own lives (personal joys, dreams, expectations, pains, fears, insecurities, demons, struggles, etc.) and develop a new understanding of their individual life situations and relationships.

In an interview with the *New York Times*, three-time Oscar-nominated actor Mark Ruffalo said of Arthur Miller's examination of economic and class struggles in *The Price*, "Art is activism. My [acting] teacher used to say: 'We should pay to go to church, and the theater should be free. That's where we learn about ourselves.'"

Not only does the audience learn about themselves from theatre, actors, through self-exploration, learn who they are as people.

‹ TERMS ›

THE FOLLOWING TERMS RELATE to the work processes and structures used by actors. They are essentials tools for actors.

ACTING: To act is to do—or, more simply, *acting is doing*. Every moment of an actor's life on stage should involve an act of doing something physical, verbal, non-verbal, or psychological.

SCORE: A term Uta Hagen used to encompass all the ingredients on which actors work when preparing to present a scene, monologue, or exercise. She derives the term from a music score and the technical ingredients that musicians must deal with in playing a piece of music.

SIX STEPS: Uta Hagen's guide of six steps (*character, circumstances, relationships, objectives, obstacles*, and *actions*) used to build and bring to life the acting score for any scene, monologue, or exercise on which actors work.

OBJECTIVE: What a character wants to achieve in life and in each scene. The goals of a character. The driving force of a character. What a character wants to accomplish.

The character's *objective* is the umbrella for all other work in a scene.

OBSTACLE: The person or thing that stands in the way of a character achieving their *objective* or prohibits a character from moving forward towards their *objective*.

There always will be *obstacles* in a play, just as there are in life. *Obstacles*, or stumbling blocks, can arise from a character's fears, inadequacies, etc. They provide conflict, a necessary ingredient in drama.

ACTIONS: What actors play in order to achieve their *objectives* and overcome the *obstacles*. *Actions* are always active verbs: *to persuade, to encourage, to demand,* etc. Actors should avoid adjectives and adverbs; they will result in playing mood, emotional qualities (sad or happy), and generalities. Verbs can be physical (*to sort* the socks), verbal (*to scold* the child), non-verbal (*to accuse* the lover with a silent inner connection to infidelity and betrayal), or psychological (*to convince* the boss).

Verbs can also be combined. For example, if my *objective* is to convince my boss to give me a raise, then my physical *action* might be to correct my posture. My verbal and psychological *actions* might be to sell my achievements. Verbs activate actors. They make the work clean, thereby enabling the audience to see exactly what actors are doing. Actors move a play from its beginning to its conclusion by playing *actions*. Note: *Some directors and teachers use the word intentions instead of actions. The terms are interchangeable.*

TRANSFERENCE: A process Uta Hagen used for personalizing the *relationships, places, objectives, actions,* and emotional life of a character. Actors use their life experience to identify and find the necessary personal behaviors of the characters they play.

For example, in *QED* by Peter Parnell, I played Richard Feynman, the real life physicist. In the play Feynman gives many lectures and speaks with great passion when he teaches physics. Likewise, when I teach acting, I speak with great passion. Therefore, I equated acting with physics, *transfered* that behavior to the text, and personally identified with Feynman. This *transference* led me to the *actions* I played in those lectures. (See Class Six for a detailed discussion of *transference*.)

◄ CREATING THE STUDIO ENVIRONMENT ►

THROUGHOUT MY CAREER, I have conducted many acting workshops, usually in a university setting. As I entered the space where I was to conduct the class, I would often discover a large empty room, most likely a rehearsal hall (or even worse, a dance studio with mirrors).

Therefore, in my basement studio in Kansas City, I have tried to replicate Uta Hagen's classroom at the HB Studio in New York: an intimate space that is free of mirrors. I don't want students looking at themselves while working. Actors need to be involved subjectively in their work, not objectively observing themselves.

Since actors require objects with which to work, the studio contains many props and set pieces: a love seat that converts to a bed, a coffee table, assorted chairs and tables, a door to enter from or exit to the outside world, a folding screen for entrances or exits to interior environments, a portable stove and sink, a desk, a small refrigerator, lamps, magazines, books, dishes, glasses, coffee mugs, eating utensils, assorted bottles (soda, beer, wine, and liquor), remote controls, various telephones, and a dysfunctional laptop. I also have created a library of plays and theatre books for students to check out and use in their studies.

In each two hour class, work is done under a microscope. Since we have the luxury of working in a near ideal environment, the pressures of opening night—or a critic's approval or disapproval—do not exist. Classes are comprised of professional actors, beginning actors, community theatre actors, and non-actors who have always been curious about acting. Some of my students will never step on stage, but in class, they gain a new respect for theatre and insights into themselves and others. I have been told by a few students that, as a result of class, they now experience their worlds differently.

For actors who are cast in plays with limited rehearsals in preparation for an opening, many pressures exist. Actors must focus on quickly learning lines and blocking, discovering *relationships*, identifying with and projecting their characters, and suspending their disbelief relative to the *circumstances* and truths of the plays.

During rehearsals, actors must use only the things learned in class that have been ingrained in their instruments. It is impossible to incorporate each and every principle discussed in class. There is not enough time. Attempting to do so will drive actors crazy and make them insecure. Actors must trust that their talents will work for them. After all, they wouldn't have been cast if the director didn't have faith in them. It is during the run of the plays when actors often work out some of the unfinished acting problems.

When I first attended professional theatre as a child and teenager, I loved *everything* I saw. But the more I have studied the craft, the less I have enjoyed watching live theatre. I found myself looking for flaws and the theatrical devices used in the attempt to cover them. Now, when I go to the theatre, I try to enjoy the experience by not viewing the production through the lens of a teacher, actor, or director. I try to recapture that childlike experience I had many years ago, but it is hard to close the doors that I worked so hard to open.

‹ Class ›

For five years I had the privilege of studying with the great actor and teacher Uta Hagen, who wrote two books on acting: *Respect for Acting* and the definitive *A Challenge for the Actor*, which I especially recommend. In Chapter Ten of the latter book, Ms. Hagen details each of the **Six Steps** with specificity. I use these steps as an actor, director, and teacher.

In my classes there are three areas of work: scenes, monologues, and the Uta Hagen exercises, which are outlined in the following chapter. All work is rehearsed outside of class and brought into class for evaluation. I have also designed a series of improvised exercises, which are done in class, to demonstrate and clarify specific acting problems and techniques.

Scenes and monologues are used to test the principles of the work explored by actors in the exercises. Actors should come to each class with one piece of rehearsed work. If for some reason actors are unable to prepare something for class, it should not prevent them from attending. They will learn by watching others and relating those acting problems to their own. I typically assign an improvisation or exercise, which is focused on specific acting problems, to unprepared actors, thereby ensuring their active participation in the class.

When actors bring in a piece of work for evaluation, it should not be thought of as a performance. A performance requires, among other things, a director. Using the *Six Steps*, the focus of actors should be on discovering the personal, organic behaviors of their characters. I evaluate work from the actors' perspectives, and based on that evaluation, it will be reworked for the next class.

Actors should not direct themselves or their partners, including blocking: the physical movements of the characters in the scene. Physical movements should happen organically and evolve from discoveries of a character's needs, *objectives*, *actions*, *obstacles*, and *relationships*. These discoveries will result in specific physical destinations. Actors should avoid aimless wandering, pacing, and posing for theatrical effect.

Even though it may seem obvious, actors must check the impulse to help their partners by offering suggestions. It is important for actors to make discoveries themselves. By observing their partner's work, actors lose subjectivity, thus doing themselves a disservice by becoming objective in the life of the scene. When actors attempt to make the scene more interesting, dramatic, funny, etc. by thinking about how the audience will respond (or by intentionally eliminating the *obstacles* of the scene), actors can consciously (or subconsciously) stack the cards in a character's favor, which defeats the purpose of scene work.

Actors should resist showing their work to friends, husbands, wives, lovers, or other theatre people. Since everyone has an opinion about acting, they will offer suggestions—and maybe even demonstrate how to play it. Actors want to succeed and are often looking for approval. Therefore, most actors will accept these sincere but misguided suggestions and aim for the performance rather than the process. When this occurs in class, we, unfortunately, have to go back to square zero and start all over.

As actors work to develop their craft and grow as artists, the studio serves as a laboratory for discovery where actors can trust both themselves and me. In the studio I encourage actors not to compare themselves to other actors. Each actor is unique and not comparable. In class actors have the right to be god-awful and boring. It's the perfect place to exercise this right. Remember, we all have been there. It is part of the learning process.

Scenes should be short: five minutes max. Actors should time scenes before bringing them to class. Monologues and exercises should be two to three minutes. Recreating life is a huge acting problem, which is plenty for an actor to do in a few minutes of work. In short scenes we can pinpoint problems much easier than we can in long scenes, where so many problems may exist that we don't know where to start. In long scenes actors typically go for the performance, working to get to the emotional climax of the scene. The studio should not be used as a substitute for a performance experience.

I don't direct actors in the work. But I do point out two or three specific areas of focus (such as *place, objective, character, relationships,* etc.) in the scene, monologue, or exercise that need to be developed or rethought in relation to the acting score and explored differently for the next class. I also try to point out possible bad acting conceptions, habits, mannerisms, tricks, etc. If I provide actors with more than two or three suggestions, then I run the risk of confusing them and leaving them with no idea of where to start the rework. Occasionally, I will work with actors on a specific moment of the scene, thereby demonstrating for the entire class how to solve a particular dramatic problem. I don't try and teach all of the rehearsal procedures in the first class; they are covered as teaching points in each of the six classes and evaluations.

◄ THE REHEARSAL PROCESS ►

FIRST, ACTORS NEED TO choose a scene or monologue on which to work. Once the scene or monologue has been selected, actors must read the entire play, not just their scene or monologue. The first reading is done as an audience member or as a student of literature. In subsequent readings actors should explore the play as a worker involved in the process of bringing the scenes to life.

Throughout the rehearsal process, actors need to read the play as many times as possible. In order to make acting choices that fulfill the needs of the play, it is important that actors understand the play and what the playwright is saying.

During the first rehearsal of a scene, actors should read the scene for content while resisting the urge to perform or impress. Next, in the second read, actors—through seeing and listening from their characters' points of view (needs, *relationships, objectives*)—can make simple connections to each other.

In real life we listen to the content of what is being said and how that content relates to our needs, *relationships, objectives*, and values. We also visualize what is being said to us. This does not mean that we hear each individual word.

NOTE TO ACTORS: Focus on your partner. In a scene the other actor is more important than you. They provide your next moment of life. While your partner is reading their dialogue to you for the first time, don't look ahead to your next line. Stay visually connected to your partner and listen. If you lose your place in the text, that's okay. Don't worry about picking up cues or timing. Just listen and stay in the moment. Acting is not only about words; it's also about the totality of life. Words are only one aspect of this process.

Use your imagination. Place yourself in the given *circumstances* of the play, and look for your own human response to what is happening in the scene. You are a human being, and who you are is your acting instrument. There is not another instrument like yours; it is your trademark, your product. Use it. Just because Billie Holiday does not sing a song the same way as Judy Garland or Edith Piaf, it does not mean that each version isn't still exciting and emotional to listen to: each performer projects their life experience into the lyric. The song becomes personal, and we empathize and identify with the humanity each artist reveals. In my opinion good acting does the same.

The dictionary defines character as the "combined moral or

ethical structure of a person." Therefore, forget your ideas about the character. Through personal identification, you will find the character in you. The term "my character" is not only possessive in nature but also includes your personal understanding and empathy. "My character" is mine; it is coming from me. The character is me.

When thinking or talking about your character, use the pronoun "I" instead of "she" or "he" or "they." It will help you confront the *circumstances* in the play.

As actors, we are attempting to bring real life to the stage. We are not pretending to be someone else. Keep this simple fact in mind as you repeat the visual-contact method of reading a scene.

And as the rehearsal process progresses, the visual contact between you and your partner will change. There will be situations when the focus of your visual attention shifts to different objects for various purposes, and other times, it will be necessary for you to avoid looking at your partner at all.

◄ BEATS ►

A BEAT IS WHERE something begins and then changes in a scene—where something is accomplished, defeated, deferred, interrupted, or dropped. Let's explore the first beat of a specific example. In Act One, Scene Two of the classic American comedy *You Can't Take It with You* by Moss Hart and George S. Kaufman, Alice, the youngest daughter in the Sycamore family, has returned home with her new boyfriend, Tony, after a late date. Since neither wants the night to end, this scene is not unlike the balcony scene in *Romeo and Juliet*.

Much like the Nurse in *Romeo and Juliet*, family members are constantly interrupting Tony and Alice. In both plays families are *obstacles*.

Alice's family is lower middle class, and their priorities are simple. Tony's family is wealthy (Wall Street money), conservative, and active in elite society. These aspects of the work deal with the acting problems of *relationship, objectives, obstacles, place, action,* and historical reality.

As the couple approaches Alice's dark house, save a light in the hall, their voices drift through.

> ALICE (*off stage*)
> I could see them dance every night of the week. I think they're marvelous.

> TONY
> They are, aren't they? But of course just walking inside any theatre gives me a thrill.

> ALICE
> Well, it's been so lovely, Tony, I hate to have it over.

> TONY
> Oh, is it over? Do I have to go right away?

> ALICE
> Not if you don't want to.

> TONY
> I don't.

> ALICE
> Would you like a cold drink?

The first beat ends on Tony's line, "I don't," and the second beat begins with Alice's line, "Would you like a cold drink?" In this example both characters get what they want: Tony gets to stay a little longer, and Alice, who comes from a different cultural and economic background, which she considers an *obstacle* to this *relationship*, is able to hold on to the fantasy of a life with him.

This play, a period piece set in 1936, is considered historical, i.e., it does not take place in the present. Therefore, actors need to research what was happening in 1936 (the U.S. was in the middle of the Great Depression) and behave *as if* it is the present. The economic conditions, fashions, politics, music, manners, films (a great resource), and sports of this period need to be embraced by actors and made personal. Tony and Alice need to relate to these things and behave *as if* they are living in 1936. Some things will be the same as present time and other things will be different. This exploration of the past is not an historical research project. By using imagination, craft, and research, an actor's goal is to create contemporary life in this world of 1936 *as if* it were the present.

For example, the actors might imagine that Tony has driven Alice home in his new car. Maybe he stops at the curb, helps her out of the car, holds her hand for the first time, and walks her up the sidewalk onto the porch. Perhaps Alice invites him in, and they walk into a dark hall where she turns on the light and begins the dialogue.

Before the entrance and dialogue, what are Tony and Alice thinking about? They have just returned from a performance of the Monte Carlo Ballet. The text doesn't tell us what ballet. Actors need to supply details that are not in the text. These details dictate the behaviors of characters and influence *relationship*, *objectives*, and *actions*. In our attempt as actors to bring real human beings on stage, we need to discover these details and allow them to send us into action. Every time actors prepare for any scene in any play, they must work on previous *circumstances*.

As actors discover who they are in a play and what is at stake for them, they need to consider what their world has been like on the particular day in which a scene takes place. Our example is a love scene that ends with Tony proposing to Alice and her accepting. Both characters are attracted to each other and have been looking forward to this evening for some time. It is their first real date. The day has finally arrived, and both Tony and Alice are excited. They have made preparations about what to wear and have great expectations about this evening.

In this scene actors need to consider what turns them on to their sexual partner and then find specific things in each other in order to pinpoint the nature of the attraction. It may be physical, emotional, psychological, intellectual, or a combination of any or all of these.

Most of us can relate to this *relationship* in a personal way from our own life experience, which is the key to personally identifying with the character. It is where the scene starts for both actors.

NOTE TO ACTORS: All of these issues are there for you to discover in the first beat of the scene. As you start work on the first beat, rehearse it over and over, each time working on specific acting problems: *objectives, obstacles, actions* (verbs), *place, relationships,* etc. Define who you are and find personal identification with your character and the given *circumstances.* You can only work on one problem at a time, which is why it is important to work the first beat several times.

While you probably won't solve all of the acting problems in your first rehearsal, try to tackle two or three of them. Then, during the next rehearsal, add on to what you have accomplished. Once you feel that you have made the necessary discoveries in the first beat, go on to the next beat, repeating that same process. As you progress in working on the scene's beats, you will deepen the discoveries you made in the first beat and find the character inside you.

At the end of your rehearsal, run what you have worked on. That's what you bring to class. You do not have to bring in the whole scene. Avoid the trap of running the entire scene over and over again in your rehearsal. This practice results in general work, whereas working in beats results in specific work. Working in beats also helps you learn the dialogue during the work process, thereby eliminating a lot of forced memorization.

Personally, I have always felt that the first beat is the most important, and difficult, in any scene. So much needs to be established in this beat. If that beat is solidly worked on, then the other beats will fall into place. Most of the considerations I have mentioned in this section have little to do with dialogue but strongly influence behavior and *relationships.* Acting is not just about words; it is about playing verbal, physical, psychological, and non-verbal *action.*

‹ PLACE ›

NEXT, ACTORS SHOULD FOCUS on *place* (environment). In *You Can't Take It with You,* the actors playing Alice and Tony need to setup the room, complete with furniture and objects. Yes, it is Alice's *place*, but since both actors have to work in the space, input from Tony is needed as well.

In one run through Alice might notice the things about the room that embarrass her and then find something to do about it. Tony, in his mind, might compare the room to the formal dining room at his home. To him, maybe the room looks comfortable and lived in. As a result, he would explore those elements of the room.

During another rehearsal focusing on *place*, Alice might move to the couch and sit down. Tony then sees this as an opportunity to get close to her. He might leave his chair at the table and join her on the couch. Soon, actors will learn that when working in this manner, discoveries— such as the one above—are not that unusual. When trying to solve one acting problem, in this case *place*, Tony's *action* has connected him to one of the other **Six Steps**: *relationship*.

In all scenes actors need to supply for themselves the specifics of time. What year is it? 1936. What month is it? June. What day is it? Thursday, June 18th. What time is it? Eleven-thirty at night. In what country, state, city, village, building, room, or landscape is the character living? Where, physically, is the character? What are the weather conditions? (See the Fourth Side [Chapter 12] and Outdoors [Chapter 16] Exercises in *A Challenge for the Actor*.)

Actors should talk about *place* but accompany the discussion with doing. *Acting is doing*. If the door is across the stage, then actors should go to the door and put their hands on it. How does it feel? What is its texture? Is it expensive or cheap, new or old? How does it open and close? Actors should do the same with furniture and objects in the room. If the scene takes place outdoors, then actors should do the same thing with what they see and contact physically.

NOTE TO ACTORS: *Place* is important. Your goal, as the character on which you are working, is to believe that you are living in the *place* described by the playwright. If you achieve this belief, then your work will have a strong foundation and allow for exploration of the other acting problems in the scene.

Consider your character's personal *relationship* to the space and its contents. Ask yourself, "Is this my *place* or someone else's? Am I comfortable here? How do I behave here? Do I really like the things here, or do I think they are ugly?"

It is important to use real objects and furniture. Do not mime things. Real objects help you believe and give you life. They increase your faith that you exist in the environment of the play and are not in a studio or on a stage in front of an audience. If a set piece, prop, or object is unavailable at the studio, then bring it from home.

A solid sense of *place* will free you, and you will lose that sense of self- and audience-awareness, thereby creating a strong sense of privacy. In other words, you will feel relaxed and behave *as if* you are not being observed. The *as if* is important since a part of you is always aware of the presence of the audience. It is our job to communicate to them.

◄ WARDROBE ►

ANOTHER CONSIDERATION OF WHICH actors need to be aware is the influence of clothing on human behavior. If the young woman playing Alice in *You Can't Take It with You* comes to rehearsal in shorts, T-shirt, and flip flops, then she is working against herself. The play is set in 1936, and Alice has just returned from the ballet with her handsome and wealthy boyfriend. She is probably wearing a dress, which costs more than she could afford, that she bought specifically for this occasion. An actor's behavior in an expensive dress is far different than their behavior in shorts, T-shirt, and flips flops.

NOTE TO ACTORS: As the character you are playing, ask yourself, "What am I wearing?" The selection of clothes you wear places you one step closer to discovering who you are in the play.

Find items in your wardrobe that will help you discover the behavior needed for your character. Thrift stores can also be a great resource to find vintage clothes and other items. If working on the character of Julius Caesar, then use your imagination and find an old bed sheet for a toga. Don't wait until the day you bring the scene to class or until the first dress rehearsal when the designer presents your "costume." A costume is not only for the audience; it's also for you, the actor. You need to work with clothing in rehearsal in order to discover the behaviors of your character.

‹ CONSTRUCTING THE BACKSTORY ›

ON THE SURFACE, CONSTRUCTING the backstory in our seemingly simple little love scene from *You Can't Take It with You* should be easy. But upon closer examination, it becomes quite complex. Actors are like detectives. We accept the *circumstances* the playwright gives us as true and then imagine and invent backgrounds for the characters we play.

For example, if I am playing Tony, an only child, then I might imagine that I attended private schools and lived away from home. Perhaps I attended an Ivy League university such as Yale, and after graduation, I took off time to travel and enjoy myself. Ready to settle down, I accepted a job at my father's Wall Street Firm and have been promoted to vice president. At work is where I meet Alice.

If I'm playing Alice, whose background is completely different, then I need to invent and imagine my own backstory. I know that I have an older sister and that our large, extended family lives with my grandfather. Perhaps I went to public schools and have never lived away from home. I took secretarial classes in school, which enabled me to find employment at Tony's father's firm, a major achievement in the on-going economic depression.

NOTE TO ACTORS: The previous examples illustrate brief sketches of each character's histories. You, as actors, must fill in the specific details in your characters' lives.

As you work through the beats, put together a backstory that works for you. Since each of you has your own background, it, therefore, is important for your character to have one as well. But make sure the choices you make enhance the play, e.g., don't make Tony an ex-convict or Alice a recovering alcoholic.

‹ IDENTIFICATION WITH CHARACTER ›

ACTOR, WRITER, AND DIRECTOR extraordinaire Orson Welles believed that the root of every good performance given by an actor comes from the actor's self. He believed that every human being is capable of committing both evil and altruistic acts and that there is a Hitler and Gandhi within all of us. I think there is truth in this assertion.

Actors need to recognize this reality in themselves. Since most of us have a favorable self-image, this ability to see the worst in ourselves does not always exist. Actors need to be aware of the selfish, vindictive, egotistical, jealous, etc. behaviors within us that make up part of who we are as humans. Awareness of these negative traits helps actors identify with characters who possess those qualities.

NOTE TO ACTORS: Look for the similarities between you and the character you are playing, and then look for the differences. In order to eliminate the differences, use your imagination and think under what *circumstances* you might behave in the same manner as your character. Examine your life experience and try to find behaviors that you have buried. Knowing yourself and coming to terms with all parts of who you are as a person will serve you as an actor. It will open the door to many different characters you can play.

‹ THE ACTORS' TECHNIQUES ›

AS ACTORS CONTINUE TO study and perform, they will develop their own ways of working, which are usually based on a compilation of techniques that they have found to work best for them. The techniques I present here are derived from what I have learned and practiced as an actor. I don't mean to imply that my methods are the only way of working. But they work for me, and hopefully, some, if not all, will serve actors and teachers as well.

Throughout my career, I have worked with actors who had never heard of *objectives* or *actions*, and they still delivered first rate performances. But the techniques I use as an actor put me in control of my work and help me sustain a performance with immediacy and spontaneity throughout the entire run of a play. These are the techniques I teach in my classes.

‹ DISCIPLINE FOR ACTORS ›

IN MY OPINION MANY actors lack rigor in their work. I have worked with actors who never learned their exact lines and paraphrased their way through opening night. Actors have a responsibility to memorize the dialogue exactly as written by the playwright, who worked hard to create characters and the exact words they use.

Another important discipline for actors is research, specifically the historical period of a play's setting, the personal identification with the characters they are playing, and the discovery of the correct choices of *action* that will best communicate what the playwright is saying and why they have written the play.

Finally, actors must be on time to class, rehearsals, and, of course, performances. In fact, they should try to arrive early. I like to arrive at the theatre at least thirty minutes before the start of rehearsal, which gives me plenty of time to organize my things, use the restroom, and review what we will be working on.

All of these things are homework for actors. Putting in only rehearsal time is not enough for actors. Much like a skilled athlete or trained musician, actors must work at perfecting their craft. According to concert violinist Pinchas Zukerman, devotion to one's craft and an intense practice schedule is crucial:

> I work my ass off every day. I practice my scales. My ongoing dedication to the profession is absolutely without any hesitation. I don't think twice about anything except making it better every day. I teach like that, I play like that and I live like that.

The same applies to actors: only through hard work, dedication, and discipline can actors turn the craft of acting into art.

CHAPTER 2

~

GUIDE TO THE UTA HAGEN ACTING EXERCISES

U TA HAGEN'S EXERCISES ARE designed to make actors
aware of their human behaviors and aid in solving the
many acting problems that come up when rehearsing
a play. Teachers and students, please refer to Ms. Hagen's book,
A Challenge for the Actor, for instructions and details about each
exercise, which should be worked on in the order they are presented
in the book. The Hagen exercises are:

1. Destination
2. The Fourth Side
3. Changes of Self: Part One & Part Two
4. Moment to Moment
5. Re-creating Physical Sensations
6. Bringing the Outdoors on Stage
7. Finding Occupation While Waiting
8. Talking to Yourself
9. Talking to the Audience
10. Historical Imagination

When working on these exercises, actors must give themselves
a *place* where the event is happening, an *objective*, and an *obstacle*
(or *obstacles*) to that *objective*. *Place* should include not only
the essential furniture and objects needed for the exercise but
everything required to complete the entire room (or if outdoors, the

environment). If actors can solve the issues of *place, objective,* and *obstacle(s)* in an acting exercise, then they will know how to solve them when they come up while rehearsing a play.

NOTE TO ACTORS: Don't worry about making the Hagen exercises dramatically interesting or humorous. That's not the point. You are not in class to entertain us, nor are you playwrights. You are actors. The simplest, everyday choices—such as folding laundry while waiting for an important phone call, planning a menu for a dinner party, working out a budget, paying bills, getting dressed for an audition, etc.—are best. They are the ones with which you are most familiar and can, therefore, identify.

The exercises are designed to explore human behavior, not emulate television or movies. So, do not create fantastical storylines that involve suicide notes, murder plots, or bank robbery plans.

In the exercises you are always yourself, not a character you invent. For many actors, this task is difficult. Many actors like to hide themselves behind—and then play—their ideas of who they think the character should be. Don't do this. According to *Hamilton* creator Lin-Manuel Miranda, if he "can find [him]self in the work, others will see themselves."

Therefore, explore and get to know your own human behavior, which most of us take for granted and think uninteresting. Awareness of your own behavior will help you identify with characters as humans and lead you to specific *actions* during rehearsal. By bringing your own human behaviors to the characters you play, you make the characters human. In the exercises your job is to focus on the acting problems present in each exercise and execute those problems in specific human terms.

When rehearsing the exercises, make choices that put you in control of the truth arising from your playing space. Use real objects and furniture, nothing imaginary. Real objects create a sense of privacy and help you lose, to a large degree, your audience awareness. A part of you will always be aware of their presence, since our job as actors is to communicate to the audience.

In the exercises, it is permissible to talk, as long as you are organically talking to yourself (as you would in real life) and not talking in order to tell the audience the story. You can also receive or make phone calls. If you want to receive a call, then ask a classmate to be your stage manager. Tell your classmate specifically where you want the phone to ring and have them cue you with, "Ring ring." This cue will help you stay in the moment and not anticipate the phone ringing.

The exercises are not improvisations. They should be rehearsed a minimum of one hour. Don't just think about an exercise as you are driving to class and then come into class and present it as an improvisation. That's not the point.

Your first rehearsal, however, will be improvised. As you continue to rehearse during the week, the exercise will gradually set itself. When you bring the exercise to class, you should know exactly what you are going to do and when you are going to do it.

I can't tell you the number of times that new students come to the second class, present the *Destination Exercise*, and when I ask them how it went in relation to their rehearsals, they reply: "I didn't rehearse it. That's what I do every day."

Yes, you may engage in those behaviors every day, but they are different every day. For example, I brush my teeth every morning, but while brushing my teeth, conditional factors can affect my behavior: waking up late after a night out and having to rush in order to make it to work on time, being nervous and having high expectations about an audition that I have later that morning, feeling concern over a large and unexpected bill, etc. On any given day while brushing my teeth, any or all of these surrounding *circumstances* influence my behavior.

So, don't present a series of activities that lack the everyday conditions that influence behavior. Rehearse the exercise with your behavior on a specific day. It should be like a carefully rehearsed scene from a play in which you are on stage by yourself for two minutes. Execute the exercise *as if* it is happening for the first time. That's the actor's challenge.

To accomplish this feat, keep your thoughts and *actions* in the present tense. The work is alive and happening *now*, even though you have carefully rehearsed it. The cliché of "living in the moment" is especially true for actors. How often have we seen a performance where it was apparent that the events were rehearsed some time ago and what we were witnessing was the outer shape of those events? Such a performance is a carbon copy of something that might have been exciting a long time ago but is now hollow.

I have become a sports fan. I enjoy the concentration, immediacy, spontaneity, skill of the players, and the fact that the live events of a game can never be repeated. Like athletes, actors must bring the same concentration, immediacy, spontaneity, and skill to their performances throughout the entire run of a play.

While working on the Hagen exercises, not only are you solving acting problems, but you are learning how to rehearse and becoming aware of your own behavior. Try spreading your rehearsals out over the week: fifteen minutes one day and fifteen minutes another day, etc. This spacing between rehearsals will provide you with thinking time and give you new ideas and choices to try in your next rehearsal.

Keep the work short, two to three minutes. In rehearsals don't forget to establish the *place* where the exercise is occurring. Creating the *place* is not for the benefit of the audience but for the benefit of you, the actor. It will relax you, give you a sense of privacy, and thereby influence real human behavior in the space while also helping you discover the *actions* (verbs) you play in order to achieve your *objective* and overcome the *obstacles*.

Soon, you will realize the great variety in your own behavior, which can be *transferred*, through personal identification, to the characters you play. These newly found behaviors will open doors to the number of characters you can play.

Each exercise should be repeated many times in subsequent classes. As you become more familiar and practiced with the exercises, you can combine the acting problems of several exercises into a single exercise.

For example, you may choose to work on the acting problems *destination, use of the fourth side,* and *talking to yourself* in a single exercise.

The exercises are useful for actors of all skill levels: from novice to seasoned stage actors. Geraldine Page, Broadway star and Academy Award winner, once returned to Ms. Hagen's class and said, "All I want to work on are the exercises."

NOTE TO TEACHERS: This book contains twenty exercises that I have created for you to use in your classes or for actors to rehearse and bring to class. Feel free to create new exercises that will help actors understand the various problems that arise in the monologues, scenes, or plays on which they are working.

By examining your behavior in everyday life (such as returning home with bags of groceries and having to use the bathroom but being unable to find the right key on your key ring to unlock the house door), you can create exercises that involve the basic acting problems: *objective, immediacy, conditions, obstacles, actions,* and *place.* If students can solve these problems in an exercise, then it should lay a strong foundation for dealing with the same problems in the context of a play.

As actors progress in the class, the scenes, monologues, and exercises on which they are working should become more complex and challenging. By repeatedly working on the exercises, actors' skills will grow. As a result, they will gain confidence and freedom in the creative choices they make when attempting to solve acting problems.

Furthermore, it is important that actors receive voice and body training, including speech and vocal production. For some students, additional training for singing, dancing, or fencing might be necessary. Partner sports such as tennis can be useful. When I studied with Ms. Hagen, she insisted that I take dance classes in order to learn how to manage the physical tension in my body.

Teaching is an art. Since it is our goal to bring to stage real, living people that are battling to overcome the many problems faced in our characters' lives, be sensitive to actors' problems and assist them in clarifying the mysteries of being human.

◄ THE MELDING OF CHARACTER AND SELF ►

IN THIS BOOK I frequently discuss the *use of self* by actors in their work. I believe the goal of the Hagen exercises is for actors to learn how to meld self and character. This melding of character and self doesn't mean that actors hide behind their characters, nor does it mean that actors only play characters *as if* they are playing themselves, although many actors work in this manner. Rather, the melding of character and self means that actors reveal parts of themselves in the characters they play.

Following a performance, an audience member approached Ms. Hagen and said, "I have seen you in many plays, and after each one, I think I know who you are. But I don't. You are different in every one."

This type of skilled work requires that actors have a deep understanding of their characters and themselves. Actors must select different elements of the self and weave those elements into their characters. As a result, they will discover personal identifications with who they are in a play and develop original interpretations of characters, thus making the work unique.

While discussing the performance of Alex Sharp in his review of *The Curious Incident of the Dog in the Night-time*, Hilton Als wrote in *The New Yorker*:

> Sharp knows that acting should be both an exploration of character and an exploration of self. But so few performers are able to pull this off that when one succeeds, it generates a deep audience wonder; how many of us can say we truly know our inner selves as well as the fictional selves we project, let alone manage to combine the two?

This exploration of character and self by skilled actors is indeed a wonder to witness. Performers that I have seen pull this off in live performances include: Uta Hagen, Marcel Marceau, Herbert Berghoff, Olympia Dukakis, Cherry Jones, Jean-Louis Barrault, Judy Garland, and Barbara Cook.

Furthermore, the melding of self and character is also exciting to work on as an actor. First, actors must have an honest knowledge of who they really are as human beings. Since each of us has many selves, I suggest that actors start rehearsals with an exploration of the self by working on areas that will help them personally identify with their characters. Then, through imagination, an understanding of character, and by playing specific *actions* (verbs), actors can release the personal traits from within themselves that reveal the identities of their characters. (See the Waiting Room Exercise in Class Five.)

When working as Meryl Streep's accompanist on the film *Florence Foster Jenkins*, Simon Helberg commented to the New York Times, "She's human. She might be one of the greatest artists we've ever had, but the reason she's so great is that she brings all of the life that's happening around her and in her to each moment." These types of moments, brought about by the melding of character and self, are what actors should strive for in each performance.

◄ FINDING A CHARACTER INSIDE THE SELF ►

ACTORS OFTEN FORGET THE one thing that they have in common with their characters: both are human. It is necessary for actors to bring that humanity to their characters. First, actors should look for the areas in which they can personally identify with their characters. This personal identification is the key for the melding process.

Many actors ignore this personal identification of character in their work and jump right to the exploration of philosophical ideas about their characters. As a result, actors end up illustrating their characters instead of presenting their characters.

For the parts of characters with which actors don't identify, the imagination can be a useful tool. Actors should contemplate the *circumstances* in which they might behave in a similar manner. By researching their characters' back stories and trying to understand why their characters behave the way they do, actors can find common ground with their characters. It is important that actors not judge the morality of their characters. Moral judgments should be left to audiences. Actors, instead, must strive to justify their characters' behaviors.

Next, actors need to discover a strong *action* score, which will reveal in them those unfamiliar character traits. Since there is more to a person than one's own self-image, actors might surprise themselves and discover unknown traits buried deep inside. Ms.

Hagen once said about herself, "I think of myself as a bright shiny apple, but inside is a rotten worm."

While playing Walter, a right-wing religious right-to-life fanatic, in the play *Keely and Du* by Jane Martin, I had to identify with character traits that were unfamiliar to me. Walter's life mission (*objective*) is to stop all abortions. His drive is all-consuming. Walter arranges to kidnap a woman—in her third month of pregnancy—on her way to an abortion clinic. He plans to take great care of the woman's health and financial security while ensuring that the child is born.

Personally, I believe in a woman's right to choose. So, what possibly did I have in common with Walter? After much thought and exploration, I was able to identify on a human level with his desire to care for the woman and child. For the zealous pursuit of his goal, I related my dedication to a social cause—such as civil rights, health care, gay rights, art funding, art in the schools, climate change, etc.—where I have an all-consuming drive. I *transferred* that energy to my work on the character, which gave me the will to pursue Walter's *objectives as if* I were dealing with my passions. Eventually, I found Walter in me.

Sometimes, active research is required. If the character is an historical figure, then actors need to delve into specific research of period, including manners, clothing, class structure, politics, etc. Additionally, actors need to explore the social and economic classes of their characters and imaginatively place themselves in the period by wearing the clothes, eating the foods, drinking the wines, or penning a letter with the proper writing utensils of that time. Delving into their characters' daily routines—such as living without plumbing, electricity, central air and heating—is a necessity. This active research—when actors imaginatively place themselves in the shoes of their characters and live in that time and place in history—can provide plenty of information about their characters that will help actors identify with and bring their characters to life from within.

For example, I once played Dillwyn Knox in the play *Breaking the Code* by Hugh Whitemore, which is based on the book *Alan Turing: The Enigma* by Andrew Hodges. Knox was a classical scholar who worked in intelligence with Alan Turing during World War II. During this time, Turing invented an electromechanical machine that cracked the German Enigma code. While Hodges' book was a helpful resource, I needed more personal information about Knox. At the Kansas City Public Library, I found a book by Penelope Fitzgerald called *The Knox Brothers*, a biography of the author's family, including her father Edmund and his three brothers, one of which was Dillwyn. The information in this book was a great resource for me. My active research had provided me with plenty of personal information about my character. I was able to identify with (and bring to life) this information, which helped me find Dillwyn Knox in me.

CHAPTER 3

~

CLASS ONE:
UNDERSTANDING OBJECTIVES

A T THE START OF the first class of a new session, I ask everyone present, both new and returning students, to tell the class a little bit about themselves: what training and experience they have (if any) and what is motivating them to take an acting class. Following introductions, I define the word *objective* (see Chapter 2, Terms) and what it means for an actor. For example, in our introductory conversations, the *objective* has been to get to know each other.

As humans, we live our lives in pursuit of goals: both long range and immediate. The characters we play also live their lives in pursuit of goals. As actors, we want to present real human beings on stage. Therefore, we need to analyze how we live our lives and ask ourselves two questions: what do we want and what are we doing to achieve that target? *Acting is doing*, and we learn about acting from life. In life, we have *objectives*. And as actors, *objectives*—the goals of our characters—are the umbrella for all the other work on a scene, monologue, or exercise.

◄ EXERCISE 1: THE NAME GAME ►

IN THIS EXERCISE WE continue exploration of the *objective*: to get to know each other. Actors are required only to remember their first names. I instruct the class to form a standing circle in the workspace. One actor (the giving actor) is selected to begin. In an attempt to achieve the *objective*, the giving actor is provided with two *actions* to execute: (1) *to walk* on an impulse to another actor in the circle; and (2) *to introduce* themselves (first name only) to that actor (the receiving actor). The receiving actor then returns the introduction to the giving actor.

The actors change places in the circle and the receiving actor now becomes the giving actor by moving to a different actor and repeating the same two *actions*. This exchange will be executed one more time with another set of actors before I add a new physical *action* to the *objective*: (3) *to touch* the receiving actor on top of the head.

Now, the giving actor repeats the previous two *actions* (*to walk* and *to introduce*) followed by the new *action* (*to touch*). After every third round, I add a new *action*: (4) *to touch* the tip of the nose; (5) *to touch* both shoulders; (6) *to take* both hands; (7) *to slap* on the butt; and (8) *to give* a big bear hug.

I provide actors with only one *action* at a time, and I let them repeat that *action* a few times before adding a new *action*. After the giving actor performs their *action(s)*, the receiving actor returns the same *action(s)* to the giving actor. Thus, the receiving actor now becomes the giving actor and selects a new actor from the circle on whom to play the *actions*.

Once the bear hug has been executed, I complete the exercise by introducing *obstacles* to the *objective*: "Actors, you are late and a cab with the meter running is waiting outside to take you to the airport for your flight to Paris." The *rush for time* and the *running meter* serve as the *obstacles* to the *objective*.

Now, the actors leave the circle and simultaneously move from one classmate to the next, completing the eight physical and verbal *actions* in an attempt to overcome the *obstacles* and achieve the *objective* (to get to know each other before leaving for Paris).

NOTE TO TEACHERS: If you see actors anticipating *actions*, then call this to their attention: "Andrew, you introduced yourself to Mary while approaching her. We want the work to be clean. Therefore, perform only one *action* at a time. Please try it again and wait until you reach your destination before introducing yourself." Or perhaps Kathy moves towards Jan, and as she introduces herself, she raises her hand to touch Jan's head. In this example, Kathy is anticipating the third *action* prior to completing the second *action*. It is important for actors to execute only one *action* at a time.

After each actor has completed all eight *actions* to the other students in class, I have the actors sit down in a circle on the floor of the workspace. Then, we talk about acting and how the three ingredients (*objective, action,* and *obstacle*) of the Name Game Exercise pertain to the structure and craft of actors. From this discussion, we arrive at a definition of acting: *acting is doing*.

‹ Exercise 2: The Mirror ›

In this exercise students work in pairs, standing and facing each other. If an odd number of students exist, then one group will have three students.

From each pairing, I select one actor to be the leader. That actor starts a simple abstract movement with their arms, and the other actor mirrors the movement. We are not trying to recreate an actual mirror that reflects opposite body parts. And actors are not trying to trick each other.

It is important for the leader to move in slow motion, so that their partner can follow the movements without difficulty. If the leader's partner cannot keep up, then the leader is moving too fast. The leader should keep the movements slow and steady.

For both actors, their entire focus needs to be on each other. The leader's *objective* is to take care of their partner, and the follower's *objective* is to mirror the leader's movements.

At given moments during the exercise, I will say, "change." The follower now becomes the leader, slowly transforming the movement, without interruption, into something different.

As the exercise continues, I gradually increase the frequency of the changes. It doesn't matter if the actors lose track of who is leading and who is following. Often, the creative energies of both actors will dictate the movements and organically eliminate the roles of leader and follower. When this happens, the exercise is really working.

It is important for the movement to remain abstract. Actors should avoid realistic choices such as shaving or putting on makeup, which become too technical to replicate. Actors should also avoid balletic or martial arts movements: the simpler the movement, the better.

This exercise is non-verbal, and it is an acting exercise, not a movement exercise. The actor leading the exercise needs to make simple, slow movement choices. The leader is giving to (and taking care of) their acting partner. Both actors are communicating and working together, and one hundred percent of each actor's focus and concentration should be on their partner.

Since theatre is a collaborative art, we are dependent on the energy and personal commitment received from our acting partner. It enables us to find our characters' next moments of life. Just as in this exercise, scene work is a dance with one character leading and the other character following. Then, as the scene progresses, very often, the follower becomes the leader.

In the Mirror Exercise actors are learning to use themselves. The actor's *self* is the first thing they have in common with any character they play. Since both actors and characters are human beings, our work must start here. The groundwork for character development starts with an actor's use of self.

Upon completion of the exercise, I always provide the actors time to discuss with each other the dynamics of the exercise: where it worked or when problems occurred. As an observer, I comment, as needed, on to how to correct problems in the work.

NOTE TO ACTORS: This exercise is about reaching out to help another human. It is not a performance. The leader's only responsibility is to guide the follower with slow transitions of movement, thereby gradually taking your acting partner into new impulses of physical movement.

For example, if you are leading and your arms have been moving in a vertical pattern and suddenly you have an impulse to open your hands and arms into a horizontal pattern, then you need to slow down the movement of your hands and gradually change them to an open position before horizontally moving your arms. When movements are executed in this manner, you are gently taking your partner with you into the new movement.

Don't worry about trying to recreate an actual mirror that reflects opposite body parts. If you raise your right arm, then your partner, who is facing you, will raise their left arm. Movements should be relaxed and easy; don't work too hard. When you work on the exercise in this manner, it can be a rewarding experience for you and your partner as well as any observers.

◄ EXERCISE 3: SIMULTANEOUS OBJECTIVES ►

THIS EXERCISE IS EXECUTED immediately after the Mirror Exercise, while the class is still paired in couples that are standing and facing each other in the workspace. I ask each participant to think of something that they want to tell their acting partner. It should be something personal they can talk about for a while.

After giving the actors a few seconds to decide what they want to communicate, I instruct them to look at each other. When I say, "Go," both actors, at the same time, start talking. Each actor has the same *objective*: communicate their story to their partner.

Actors should not listen to each other but should assume that their partner is listening to them. This exercise is the only time I will ever tell actors not to listen to their fellow actors.

If actors truly commit to their *objectives*, then their bodies will become animated, and they will exhibit a strong will for their *objectives*.

Since the Mirror Exercise is non-verbal, the purpose of the Simultaneous Objectives Exercise, therefore, is to explore verbal *objectives*. The *obstacle* in this exercise, of course, is the other actor talking at the same time. The class works on this exercise simultaneously. After a minute or two, I stop the exercise, and the actors discuss with each other how they felt.

◄ EXERCISE 4: DESTINATION IMPROVISATION ►

THIS IMPROVISATION IS BASED on Uta Hagen's Destination Exercise. New students make an entrance into a room of their choice, utilizing the furniture and objects (props) provided by the studio. The *objective* of the exercise is to leave a note for someone and then exit. This exercise allows new students to become familiar with the furniture and objects in the studio.

For the entrance, actors must know the following things: (1) where they are coming from; (2) what they have been doing there; (3) why they are coming into this room (the *objective*); (4) who they are leaving the note for; and (5) why they are leaving the note. All physical movement in the room should be with purpose and destination. Actors should focus on bringing involvement from an immediate, previous *circumstance* on stage with them and then exit with involvement in a future activity.

For the exit, actors need to know where they are going and why they are going there (the *objective*). Therefore, via both an entrance and an exit, life in the present is influenced by what has happened in the past and what will be happening in the future.

In her book, *A Challenge for the Actor*, Ms. Hagen quotes director Arthur Hopkins, who said, "The reason for walking is destination!" While working with the concept of destination, actors should realize that they are moving the play from its first destination to its last destination, from its beginning to its conclusion.

By placing their focus on what to do in relationship to the (in most cases) imagined previous *circumstance*, this exercise benefits entering actors and helps them overcome their nerves. As a result, actors can channel their nervous energy directly into *actions* that are related to the previous *circumstance*. So, instead of waiting to get involved after they are on stage, actors are immediately involved in the play when they enter.

For example, suppose I am off-stage waiting for my cue to enter, which is an in-coming call on my cell phone that has been placed on the coffee table in the living room. I have decided that my previous *circumstance* is washing dishes in the kitchen. When I hear the phone ring, which has been prearranged with a classmate who will act as stage manager and provide a verbal "ring ring" cue, I might wipe (the *action*) my hands on a towel, or on my pants, just before, or as, I enter the living room.

Once on stage, I answer the phone. It is my agent asking if I can get to Gardner Sound Studio right away for a voice over job (my *objective*). I reply, "Yes. I'll be there in ten minutes." Quickly, I hang up the phone, find a scrap of paper and a pen on the coffee table, and scribble a note (the *action*) to my life partner Atif, informing him where I have gone.

When I reach for my keys (the *action*), I discover that they are not in my pocket, which is where they are supposed to be (an *obstacle*). I think to myself (another *action*), "Where could they be? In near panic I run (another *action*) back to the kitchen (off-stage) to see if I left them on the counter. Unable to find the keys, I re-enter, go to the coffee table, lift the magazines, and shake them (more *actions*) in hope that my keys might fall out. But they are not there. So, I move towards the couch, lift one of the cushions, and find them (the keys have been preset in the couch cushion prior to starting the exercise). Apparently, the keys had fallen out of my pants earlier in the day when I was sitting on the couch reading. I breathe a sigh of relief and head for the door to exit to my voice over job.

Thus, by drying my hands before coming on stage, I have entered the play with involvement from the past. Then, on stage, I am able to deal with the immediacy of the present: answering the phone, writing the note, and finding my keys. Once my keys are found, I can then make a hurried exit to the future, thinking about how much money I will make from the voice over.

Therefore, the key to this exercise is the fact that I am in action as I enter the room, am in action while I'm in the room, and am in action as I exit the room. *Acting is doing.*

◄ EXERCISE 5: THE KNOWN AND THE UNKNOWN ►

THIS EXERCISE IS AN improvisation with two actors that focuses on *relationship, place, objective,* and *obstacle*. In all improvised exercises, actors should use their own names, not made up character names. As the name of the exercise states, one actor knows everything and the other actor knows nothing. The actor who knows nothing discovers their *objective* as a result of it always being in conflict with the *objective* of the actor who knows everything.

Typically, I pair an experienced actor, Mary (the knowing actor), with a beginning actor, Sam (the unknowing actor). In a private conversation with Mary, we discuss three acting problems:

1. *Relationship* (What is their *relationship*?)
2. *Place* (Where are they?)
3. *Objective* (What are their *objectives*?)

During our discussion, Mary decides *relationship*, *place*, and *objective*. In her scenario Mary is Sam's mother (*relationship*). Sam is in the living room of their home, reading a magazine (*place* and *activity*). He wants to go to a party tonight (*objective*), but Mary has learned from a friend that there will be under-age drinking and drugs at the party. Therefore, she doesn't want him to go, which is her *objective* and Sam's *obstacle*. Sam's *objective* is that he wants to go to the party. His *objective* is always going to be in conflict with Mary's *objective*.

Mary creates *place* by setting up the studio space with a couch, coffee table, magazines, books, and a chair. It is important that Sam has something to do. Actors should never be put on stage without something to do. Mary instructs Sam to sit on the couch and read a magazine, which is not his *objective*. It is his *activity*.

At this point, all Sam knows is that he is sitting on a couch, reading a magazine. Mary has all of the information and will attempt to reveal it to Sam through verbal, non-verbal, physical, and psychological *action*. Sam will work to discover *relationship*, *place*, *objective*, and his *obstacle*.

When Mary starts the scene, Sam is the follower, just as in the mirror exercise. When he picks up on *relationship*, *place*, or *objective*, he can develop the scene with her, using the information provided from her to develop verbal, non-verbal, physical, and psychological *action*.

MARY

All right, Sam. It is settled. I've talked it over with your father, and there is no way you are going to go tonight.

SAM

Oh, yes I am.

Sam now knows that his *objective* is to go somewhere tonight. He does not know where, but hopefully, he will find out as the exercise progresses. He also possibly knows that Mary is his mother. It is important that Sam doesn't play-write. For example, if Sam said, "But Mom, I have to go. My boss is expecting me," then he would be inventing plot to serve his *objective*. Sam can only use information that he has obtained from Mary. He must follow her lead.

Much like a jazz musician or chess player must function within the rules of their respective art or game, Sam must function within the rules prescribed by his acting partner. Nadia Boulanger, the famous music composition teacher of many prominent twentieth century composers, said, "All art needs boundaries." Sam, therefore, needs to function within the boundaries established by Mary and find openings to pursue his *objective* within the rules of the exercise.

So, if Sam brings up his boss, then I stop the scene and explain to Sam that he is playwriting, which falls outside the rules of the exercise. The scene can then continue.

NOTE TO TEACHERS: This exercise contains five teaching points:

1. Are the actors, who are dependent on each other, working together?
2. Is the beginning actor able to accept the given *circumstances* as true?
3. Does the beginning actor understand their *objective* and can they play *actions* related to it?
4. Is the experienced actor, without creating exposition and telling a story, making active choices in order to reveal *relationship*, *place*, and *objective*.
5. Do both actors have strong wills for their *objectives*?

Mary's verbal life should be normal. She is not trying to conceal information and can say anything that she would say organically, without storytelling, in a real life situation. In this exercise, actors need to avoid storytelling. Below is an example of storytelling:

> MARY
> Sam, I have talked it over with your father, and as your Mother, I am telling you that, no matter what you say, you are not going to that party in the bad part of town where there will be under-age drinking and drugs.

Mary can tell Sam that he cannot go to the party, but it becomes storytelling when she invents the fact that the party is "in the bad part of town." It is also important that Mary not ask Sam any questions. It is not a guessing game. For example, I don't want Mary to say, "Sam, what are your plans for tonight?" Since Sam has no knowledge of the scene other than what he has learned from Mary, answering questions like this will force him to play-write.

If, at any time, I think the actors are in trouble or I believe that both actors clearly understand the exercise and are functioning organically, then I stop the scene. The actors' *objectives* do not have to be resolved. I then ask Sam several questions.

ME: What is the *relationship* between you and Mary?

SAM: She is my mother.

ME: Where are you?

SAM: At home, in the living room.

ME: What is your *objective*?

SAM: I want to go to the party.

Finally, I comment on three things: (1) the *actions* played by both actors in relationship to their *objectives*; (2) Mary's choices of *actions* used to reveal information to Sam; and (3) how Sam received that information and sent it back to Mary in counter *actions*. When the exercise is working properly, it functions *as if* it were a game being played by two highly skilled players.

◄ ASSIGNMENT FOR NEXT CLASS ►

AT THE END OF class, I present new students with a handout I have written about the class, which includes Uta Hagen's **Six Steps**, a guide to building their acting score, and her first two exercises: Destination and The Fourth Side. Sometimes, I ask new students to stay after class and watch a video, *Uta Hagen's Acting Class,* which demonstrates the execution of these exercises. I also encourage students to purchase her book, *A Challenge for the Actor.*

For next class, the assignment for new students is the Destination Exercise. When they bring it to the next class, it should be rehearsed.

Finally, I discuss with the students who have studied previously with me what they will be working on in terms of scenes, monologues, or Hagen exercises and offer suggestions as needed.

◄ A FINAL THOUGHT ►

DEPENDING ON THE SIZE of the class, there may not be enough time to complete all five exercises. If I am running short on time, then I usually jump to Exercise Five: The Known and the Unknown and try to work on the other exercises in subsequent classes.

Of the six classes of each session, I have found this class, the first class, to be the most challenging to teach. The difficulty lies in learning where the new students are coming from and then finding how best to integrate them into the existing class. It is why I have so many exercises. If one exercise isn't working, then I move on to another one. In an academic environment with shorter classes, the exercises of this class can be spread over several sessions.

CHAPTER 4

~

CLASS TWO:
PERSONALIZING OBJECTIVES

FOLLOWING THE FIRST CLASS and the work on the exercises, actors should have a basic understanding of *objectives*. We begin class with a review of the definition of *objectives*: what a character wants to achieve in life and in each scene of a play; the goals of a character. But for actors, intellectually understanding *objectives* is not enough. We must work towards personalizing *objectives*.

The pursuit of an *objective* has to be all consuming and needs to be absorbed into every fiber of actors: head, heart, soul, guts, etc. If actors are working correctly in rehearsal (and taking thinking time away from rehearsal), then this discovery will gradually happen over time. Thinking time away from rehearsal is important; it adds fuel to the next rehearsal.

Furthermore, actors must believe that the world of the play is their world—that the needs, desires, faults, relationships, and goals of their characters are their own. Then, and only then, can *objectives* become personal.

In this class, new students present work on the Destination Exercise, and returning students present work on scenes, monologues, and exercises. If time permits, we will review Exercise Five: The Known and the Unknown from Class One.

First, I start each class with a group exercise, which helps the students relax and focus on specific areas of concentration while also improving their ensemble work.

‹ EXERCISE 6: THE LEADER AND THE DETECTIVE ›

IN THIS EXERCISE THE entire class forms a standing circle in the workspace. I ask one actor (the detective) to leave the circle and wait patiently off stage. While that actor is away from the circle, I select a group leader. With only their arms and hands, the leader starts a very simple movement (the *action*). The actors in the circle mirror the leader's movement.

Once the leader and the class are functioning in unison, I call the detective, who had left the stage, back into the room and instruct them to enter the center of the circle. The detective's *objective* is *to detect* who the leader is by spontaneously discovering variations in the *actions* of the group.

From time to time, the leader should subtly change the movement (but only after repeating the previous movement at least four or five times). The detective's *actions* come through observation as they attempt *to figure out* from what part of the circle the new changes are coming, *to notice* actors who are not keeping up with the changes, *to scrutinize* actors' faces and observe signs of bluffing, *to catch* the leader making a change, etc.

The actors in the circle also have an *objective*: to keep the detective in the center of the circle. While following the leader, actors seek to overcome the problem of making choices that mirror the leader without focusing their attentions directly on the leader. If everyone looks directly at the leader, the detective will know immediately who the leader is.

I cannot stress enough the importance of concentrating on the *objectives*. If actors place all of their energy on the *objective*, then they will lose self-consciousness and thereby gain a freedom that allows them to discover *actions* and make creative choices in relation to the *objective*. Each actor's energy must always be moving in a positive direction towards the *objective*. Actors must make it important to achieve the *objective*.

If the detective allows negative energy to affect concentration, then self-consciousness will result, thereby creating additional *obstacles* to the *objective*. The detective should not think about how long it is taking or how many mistakes they have made. And they shouldn't compare themselves to other actors in the class, e.g., the student who selected the leader on the first try. Self-derogatory jokes from the detective are wasted energy and should be discouraged since they have nothing to do with the *objective*.

It doesn't matter if the detective's *objective* is achieved. This exercise isn't about winning. It is about focus, commitment, and concentration on the *objective*. After all, some of the greatest characters in dramatic literature never achieve their *objectives*.

The detective has three attempts to discover the leader. If the *objective* is achieved before the three guesses have been expended, then I ask the detective how they discovered the leader. I encourage the detective to divulge the various *actions* they played in order to make that determination. Sometimes actors are intellectually unable to justify their choice of the leader but intuitively felt that the leader was a certain player. I always encourage actors to trust their instincts.

The actor who plays the detective is on the spot, just as all actors are when they walk on stage. Therefore, when discussing this exercise with the students, it is important to talk about concentration and the personalization of *objectives*, *actions*, and *obstacles*. As characters struggle to overcome their *obstacles*, conflict—a necessary element in drama—is created. *Obstacles* and conflict make a play interesting.

In this exercise separate *obstacles* exist for each of the different roles of the participants:

1. For the detective, the fact that the other actors are doing the same movement;
2. For the leader, deciding when to change the movement without being obvious;
3. For the actors in the circle, discovering how to follow without looking at the leader.

For the next round, the actor who was the leader now becomes the detective. Once they leave the stage, a new leader is appointed. When the new leader starts a movement and the class is functioning in unison, I call the detective back into the room, instruct them to enter the center of the circle, and the exercise continues.

‹ A NOTE ON EVALUATIONS ›

AFTER THE OPENING EXERCISE, actors present scenes, monologues, and Hagen exercises for evaluation. After work has been presented, I always ask the actors how they felt. Did they feel good or not so good? If the work feels right, then there is a good chance that they are on the right track.

It is important for actors to learn how to develop an honest evaluation of their work. They need to be able to understand where they were working well and where they had trouble. By working with their understanding of craft, trusting their instincts and sensations, believing in the given *circumstances* of the scene, monologue, or exercise, and experiencing true involvement with their partners, actors can more easily evaluate their work.

Sometimes, I ask actors what specifically they worked on during their rehearsals. And in terms of those problems, I comment on what issues I saw and what I thought was working well. Actors need encouragement and confidence. When things are working well, I encourage actors to keep going in that direction.

Next, I ask the following questions about areas of the work that I felt needed further definition:

1. Who are you as the character? What are you wearing? What is your character's personal history? Are you finding identification with the character?
2. What do you want, and why do you want it (*objective*)?
3. What or who is in your way (*obstacle*)?
4. What do you do to overcome the *obstacles* and achieve your *objective*? What verbs are you playing (*actions*)?
5. Where are you in terms of *place* (definition and personal relationship to environment)?
6. What are your *relationships* to the other characters and the things around you?
7. What time is it (year, month, day, and time of day)?
8. Do all of your choices relate to needs of the play?

All of these issues are found in Ms. Hagen's **Six Steps** and directly relate to an actor's personal analysis and identification with the text. If an actor is having trouble with any of the eight questions listed on the previous page, then I try to offer possible considerations and suggestions as to where they can look for answers.

Finally, I give actors two or three of these problems to work on during subsequent rehearsals while preparing for the next class. It is important not to confuse or frustrate actors by giving them too many things on which to work.

◄ A NOTE ON MONOLOGUES ►

UTA HAGEN BELIEVED THAT a monologue is a scene where the character is on stage either talking to themselves or narrating to the audience. She is right. But since most actors need contrasting monologues for auditions, the task of finding monologues that fit under Ms. Hagen's definition is hard. Currently, it is standard practice for actors to use any long speech, even when a character is talking to another character, as a monologue.

In my class I ask actors to find personal *transfers* for the other, unseen character and place that person on the fourth side of their environment, behind the audience. Actors should not place the other character in an empty chair in the environment of the scene. Also, actors should not look at the person (or people) for whom they are auditioning unless specifically directed to do so.

◄ EVALUATION 1: *THE WOOLGATHERER* (MONOLOGUE) ►

AT THE END OF Class One, Greg was assigned Cliff's monologue from *The Woolgatherer* by William Mastrosimone. The play centers around two neurotic people, Rose and Cliff, in search of love. I call on Greg to present his monologue to the class. He stands in the center of the bare workspace and delivers the entire, four-page speech.

ME: Greg how did you feel?

GREG: Good.

ME: What felt good about it?

GREG: The whole thing.

ME: What really felt good was that you got through it without having to call for lines. You are to be commended for that achievement. Since it was the first time working with this monologue, I was only expecting you to bring in the first few beats. For next week, I only want you to rework the first three beats of the monologue ... that's all. Here's what I want you to work on: *place*. Today, you stood in the center of the studio reciting the monologue. As Cliff, where are you in the play?

GREG: Rose's apartment.

ME: Okay. Then you need to think about the following questions. Where is this apartment geographically? What country, state, city, or town? Where is the apartment building? What part of town? On what floor does she live? How many rooms are in the apartment? What room are you in? Are you standing on wood, carpeting, linoleum, or what? What year, month, day, and time is it? What is the temperature in her apartment? Have you been here before? What kind of furniture and objects does she have? How do you feel about being here, and what are you expecting? And finally, what is your *objective*?

GREG: I want to get laid.

ME: What is stopping you?

GREG: She is. She's crazy. She keeps diverting me. She thinks my life as a truck driver is wonderful and free. That's why I start the monologue.

ME: Getting laid may have been your initial *objective*. This monologue comes quite a ways into the play. I think your *objective* may have changed at this point. This monologue is about you and your screwed up life. Rethink your *objective*. Now let's get back to *place*. Right here in the studio, you need to construct the room from the play. Then, in the room, as Cliff, find your physical and psychological behavior. It is for your benefit, not the audience's.

GREG: But when I audition, I won't have all that stuff.

ME: True. But when you have discovered your behavior in that room here in the studio, you will be able to use the space at the audition differently. The space, as Cliff, will be yours. Most actors use the space at auditions as if they are a guest. That's what you did today. You stood in the center of the studio and said words.

If you work the way I am asking you to, then you will have ownership of the space. Acting is not just about the words; it is about the life under the words. The words come from that life.

Herbert Berghof said, "Words are the messenger of the soul." You memorized the words but did not get underneath them. As you work on the monologue this week, I want you to ask yourself this question: "Who am I as Cliff?" Today, you only worked on your ideas about him. You used your idea of what you thought was a "truck driver accent." That's not necessary. The character isn't written that way.

Next week, I want you to use yourself. Keep in mind, Cliff is a truck driver, and he hates his job. Have you ever had a job that you didn't like?

GREG: Oh yes.

ME: Okay. That's a start. Remember, we are all human beings, and all of us have had many life experiences. Use those experiences to understand and identify with your character.

Greg, think about your job and the things that you hated about it. When you are working on this monologue, equate those things to Cliff's truck driving job. *Transfer* those behaviors to the monologue. The jobs may be different, but the humanity of each job is the same. Once you do this, you will begin to identify with Cliff.

For next week, work on only the first three beats of the monologue. And focus on three of the **Six Steps**: *place*, rethink your *objective*, and find Cliff inside of you. Any questions?

GREG: No, I don't think so.

ME: If you do, then ask me before you leave … or feel free to email me.

Greg did not return to class.

‹ EVALUATION 2: DESTINATION EXERCISE ›

NEW STUDENTS PRESENT THE Destination Exercise, which has been rehearsed outside of class during the week. Jan, an 80-year-old new student, volunteers to do her rehearsed Destination Exercise. Her set consists of a living room and a bathroom. From off stage, we hear her say, "Thank you very much. You have been very kind." Jan then enters, dressed in a black tailored suit. An American flag is folded under her left arm. She places the flag on the couch, takes off her jacket, and puts it next to the flag. Next, Jan sits down on the couch, removes a mobile phone from her purse, and calls a friend.

> JAN
> Bobbie, thank you. I am really tired, and I think I am just going to stay here. (She listens.) Thanks. We'll talk soon.

She puts the phone back in her purse and walks to the bathroom, where she takes off her bracelets and sets them on a table. For a moment, she struggles with her necklace, trying her best to unclasp it, but it won't come undone.

Next, while looking into an imaginary mirror that she placed on the fourth side, Jan puts curlers in her hair, uses cold cream on her face in an attempt to remove makeup, and wipes her face with a towel. She then spends a moment in thought.

Satisfied with her bathroom accomplishments, she returns to the living room, sits down on the couch, grabs her phone, and calls back her friend.

JAN
Bobbie, I have changed my mind. If is not too late, I would like to come over. (She listens.) Okay. I will be there in about twenty minutes.

Now, with a sense of urgency, Jan removes the curlers and brushes her hair. She reaches into her purse, takes out a compact, and applies makeup to her face. As she heads for the door, Jan puts on her jacket and grabs her purse. But before exiting, she puts her left hand to her lips, kisses her fingers, and touches the flag.

ME: Jan, how did you feel?

JAN: Nervous. I was so nervous!

ME: Your focus and concentration on your *objective* and your *actions* got you through it. Your nerves did not interfere, nor were they communicated. Your entrance and exit—and all of the movement in and between the two rooms—had purpose. And your destinations were clear. You brought the play on stage with you from the past, and when you entered, you were involved in the present and existed in that reality until your exit to the future. You had destination. And your work with objects was good. You had trouble with the necklace?

JAN: Yes! I couldn't get the damn clasp undone. That never happened in rehearsal.

ME: Uta Hagen said, "If I ever have to thread a needle on stage, I want a needle with the biggest eye in show business."

Seriously though, you tackled many acting problems. Your work on inner objects—your thoughts—was wonderful. It was a perfect example of communicating without words. Your sense of *place* was good. It was yours. You were comfortable in the space and had a sense of privacy. Jan, you should feel good about your work here today. You can move on to the next Hagen exercise or work on a scene or monologue. The choice is yours. Think about it, and let me know before the end of class. I will help you find something.

Please keep in mind, the Destination Exercise is for the actor, not the audience. While it is not important for the audience to know where the actor is coming from when they enter, actors should know exactly where they are coming from since it will bring them on stage with involvement in the play.

Furthermore, this exercise helps me know if new students comprehend the principles we explored in the first class. It gives me an idea of how they work as actors.

During the Destination Exercise, I look for the following things:

- Was the actor merely indicating *action* or really executing *action*?
- Was the entrance specific or general?
- Did the physical movement in the scene have purpose?
- Was the exit specific or general?

Depending on the results of the exercise, I will either assign a scene or monologue on which the new student can start working (as I did with Jan) or have them rework the Destination Exercise for the following class. If a student does not want to work on a scene or monologue, then they can work on the remaining Hagen exercises.

NOTE TO TEACHERS: When watching this exercise, if you see actors continually enter with a prop connected to the previous *place* and activity, then there is a good chance that the actor is doing this for your benefit or the benefit of the audience. When actors do this the first time, I usually don't comment since they are at least thinking about where they are coming from.

In some scenes and plays, a specific prop is indicated by the playwright or director. But in most plays, the playwright's only stage direction is that the character *enters* and *exits*. Therefore, it is up to actors to make choices and decide from where they are coming and to where they are going. For an entrance, in most cases, actors need to find a physical *action*—something that can be executed *off stage*—relating to an activity in which the character was involved prior to the entrance cue. Please refer to my example in Class One: "I have been in the kitchen washing dishes, and before I enter, I wipe my hands on my pants." For an exit, the inner thoughts of actors should be connected to where they are going and for what purpose they are going there.

◀ EVALUATION 3: *THE LADY OF LARKSPUR LOTION* (SCENE) ▶

ELLEN AND JUDY BRING in a scene from *The Lady of Larkspur Lotion* by Tennessee Williams. Ellen is playing Mrs. Wire, the landlady, and Judy is playing the Lady. The Lady has named herself Mrs. Hardwick Moore. She claims that she is waiting for a check from her rubber plantation in Brazil, but in reality, she is turning tricks to survive.

ME: How did you feel?

ELLEN: I felt static. I didn't know what to do or where to go in her room.

JUDY: I felt terrible. I felt self-conscious.

ME: You both have provided a good evaluation of your work, which is a step in the right direction. You did a good job setting up the *place*. The faded pillows on the bed, the scarves, the boa over the back of the chair, and the box of costume jewelry on the bureau were all good choices.

Judy, the long flowing bathrobe is perfect. All of the choices you made show that you have a good understanding of the play. We see the Lady's attempt to find beauty in this hell-hole in New Orleans. But today, the objects and clothing were only decorations. They need to be a living part of the scene.

Ellen, you knocked on the door, and Judy, you took a quick swig from your bottle of cheap gin before hiding it. That was an excellent choice. It was the one place where you did bring the objects into the scene to serve you. We need more of that. Instead, you opened the door, retreated to the bed, and sat down.

Ellen, your *objective* is to collect back rent from the Lady. Since your tenants are prostitutes, alcoholics, and drug addicts, you have seen and heard it all. You must have a strong will for your *objective*. Don't forget to create a history for yourself as Mrs. Wire. What's your first name? Where is Mr. Wire? How did you end up here? See if your character has other colors. It would be interesting if you could reveal another level of Mrs. Wire.

When you entered the room, you stood by the door throughout most of the scene. You need to activate *place*. It is your house. It is your bed, night table, bureau, chairs, etc. You have ownership. You can do anything you want here because it is your *place*. The Lady is renting this furnished room from you, and she is behind on her rent. Check things out. In the scene you discover a bottle of larkspur lotion. Do you know what it is?

ELLEN: Some kind of hand lotion?

ME: No. You should look it up. It is important, especially since the title of the play is *The Lady of Larkspur Lotion*. As the landlady of this flop house, you have seen many bottles of larkspur lotion. Is the Lady a good tenant? Is she taking care of your things? Is there anything of hers that you could sell if she doesn't come up with the rent? Find things to do that will activate you. It is not just about the words. *Acting is doing.*

Judy, you are playing the Lady. You are a lady and need to construct a specific history of where you came from and how you ended up here. This play is an early William's one act. It could be considered a character study for Blanche in *A Streetcar Named Desire*. Perhaps you came from a genteel background like Blanche.

Try owning the room. I would avoid sitting. Use that great bathrobe, and experiment with the boa. Find things to do with the objects you brought in from home. Use them for comfort, reassurance, and escape.

Some verbs that come to mind are *to pull rank*, *to dramatize*, and *to fantasize*. Look for others. You, as the lady, have no money and are trying to avoid the past due rent payment by blaming and shaming the landlady for the flying cockroaches in the room. Play those verbs (*to blame* and *to shame*) in order to shift the focus from the late rent to the filthy cockroaches. And try to get the upper hand with your landlady.

Today, Judy, you were on the outside. You were using a "put on" southern accent, and all of your energy was going to the words. You were listening to yourself and thus the self-consciousness you spoke of earlier. Try working on the accent away from the text. Use it in your everyday life until you are comfortable with it. A great resource for dialects is David Alan Stern, who I have used many times. Stern teaches just about any accent you will ever need. Google him, and order a southern accent CD. He not only gives you the sounds and pronunciations of words, but he also explains where the sounds resonate from physically.

Finally, Judy, you intellectually understand the *character* and your *objective*. Look for areas in yourself where you can identify with what is humanly at stake for you as the Lady. Find a time in your life when you have been desperate. We all have had this experience many times. Also, look for times when you tried to avoid a difficult situation or when you fantasized about better conditions for yourself. If you personally go to those places, then you will identify with the character.

Oscar-winning actress Viola Davis told the New Yorker, "I don't see acting as hiding ... It's about exposing [yourself in the character]. If you're not doing that, you're basically not doing anything." When you *transfer* your personal experiences to the play and your character, you will be on the road to finding the Lady in you.

To recap, Ellen, work on activating *place* and who you are as Mrs. Wire. Judy, work on making the objects serve you in the scene, becoming comfortable with the accent, and developing who you are as the Lady. There is a lot going on in this scene, and we will work on it for a while.

Judy and Ellen did two reworks on this scene. During the process, they both grew as actors. I think it was a good learning experience for them and the class.

NOTE TO TEACHERS: While I am evaluating actors and discussing with them the work they have presented, it is important for the rest of the class to remain attentive and quiet. Actors in the "audience" should pay attention to what is being discussed during evaluations and refrain from chatting with each other—it is a distraction to both me and the class. By actively engaging during evaluations, actors will learn how to address acting problems that arise when working on scenes, monologues, and exercises and thus improve their own work.

CHAPTER 5

~

CLASS THREE: PLAYING ACTIONS

I N THIS CLASS STUDENTS present work on scenes, monologues, and Hagen exercises for evaluation. Throughout the class, special attention is given to verbal, non-verbal, and psychological *action*, including our warm-up exercise.

‹ EXERCISE 7: TO BE OR NOT TO BE ›

WHEN I WAS TEACHING at Washington University in St. Louis, Morris Carnovsky, a great actor and one of the founders of the groundbreaking Group Theatre of the 1930s, was hired to play King Lear in a university production with a student supporting cast.

I invited him to speak to my class and answer questions. He graciously accepted. During the discussion, Carnovsky pointed out that his biggest problem in working with student actors is the fact that they have no idea how to play an *action* or intention in a scene. This rang a familiar bell for me, as I had experienced the same thing when I was a student, and it encouraged me to design the following exercise, as well as several other *action* exercises.

First, I instruct the actors to form a sitting circle in the workspace. For this exercise, we use the words from the first line of Hamlet's most famous soliloquy: "To be, or not to be: that is the question." One actor is selected to begin. When ready, they look at another actor in the circle and verbally send the first word ("To") to that actor. The receiving actor then sends the next word ("Be") to a different actor. This *action* continues from one actor to the next, until we reach the last word ("Question"), which is the only two syllable word in the line. Here, each syllable is treated as a separate word, i.e., "Ques" and "Tion." The entire line is repeated over and over, until the actors are comfortable with the words and a good rhythm has been established.

I cannot stress enough the importance of actors landing these words specifically on their acting partners. The words, while moving from actor to actor, must be endowed with increasing speed and power, *as if* they were a ball traveling from one person to another.

Next, I explain verbal, non-verbal, physical, and psychological *action*. For example, in all of the exercises worked on during the first two classes, we have been playing verbs, which are the part of language that expresses *action*. And *actions* are always played with active verbs, e.g., *to charm, to beg, to entice*, etc.

Now, we slow down the exercise and use active verbs (to confide, to encourage, to insist, etc.) under Shakespeare's words. It is important to avoid using adjectives and adverbs, which will lead to playing emotional moods, attitudes, and generalities. By playing active verbs in scenes, monologues, or exercise, actors will be doing specific things. *Acting is doing.*

I stay with the same verb for the entire line of dialogue before changing to a new verb. Typically, we explore six active verbs in this exercise, and after each verb, we discuss where it was successful and what problems might have arisen.

With each verb, actors need to take a moment and decide to whom (the source) they are sending the verb and for what reason: it should be personal. Then, when everyone is ready, the actor starting the new verb selects a receiving actor by looking at that actor and then playing their *action*. It should be *as if* they are playing the verb to someone personal—a mother, father, girlfriend, etc. Actors should not try, via their imaginations, to physically project the appearance of the source onto the receiving actor. For example, if my source is my good friend Joey, who I haven't seen in over thirty years, then it is *as if* I am delivering my *action* directly to Joey (*transference*), regardless of the appearance or gender of the receiving actor, i.e., I am not trying to superimpose the physical image of Joey onto the receiving actor.

Let's suppose my verb is *to confide*. Perhaps I am going *to confide* to Joey that I am gay. Therefore, when I look at one of the other actors sitting in the circle and say the first word from Hamlet's soliloquy ("To"), I am playing an *action* (*to confide*). Internally, I am connecting both to Joey and my sexuality.

This exercise introduces students to Ms. Hagen's concept of *transference*. In the previous example I have *transferred* my *relationship* (and behavior) with Joey to the actor who is receiving my verb. Please refer to the Terms section in Chapter Two for the definition of *transference* and Class 6 (Chapter Nine), where I discuss *transference* more specifically.

Let's look at another example. If I provide the verb *to teach*, then one actor might imagine teaching their eight-year-old son how to ride a bicycle. While saying their respective Shakespearian word, each actor should know specifically who they are teaching and exactly what they are teaching, which obviously will be different for each actor.

It is important that I allow students the freedom to find their own personalization and cause. I will never ask an actor who (or what) from their personal life that they are using as a source. It's none of my business and should remain private for the actor. At a public reading of her novel *Olive Kitteridge*, Pulitzer Prize winning novelist Elizabeth Strout was asked if she had a backstory for Olive. "I do," she replied. "And I would love to tell you. But I don't think I will. There's a pressure that has to build, and if I talk about it, then I can't write it. It's like putting a pin in a balloon and just popping the air out." The same applies for actors. Publicly revealing an actor's source only diminishes its value.

Therefore, actors must know, internally, who is receiving the verb and what they expect to happen as a result of playing it. The verbs played under Shakespeare's words have nothing to do with the actual meaning of his language. We are using Shakespeare's words to learn how to play action verbs as subtext behind his language.

If actors commit to playing verbs, which must be personal and have cause, then they will be in *action*. It will feel right and will produce real sensation in the actor's self—in the actor's instrument.

Many times, actors will have ideas about how the verb should be played. For example, if the verb is *to demand* and actors play it without cause or personalization, they end up shouting and shaking their fists. When engaging in these types of *actions*, actors are illustrating and playing only the outer shape of the verb. As a result, it feels, sounds, and looks hollow.

This exercise, therefore, is not about illustrating verbs; it is about a real and purposeful doing. *Acting is doing.* Just as a musician plays notes, an actor plays verbs, whether it is in a scene, monologue, or exercise. We use verbs under the dialogue (and non-verbal moments of a scene) in order to achieve our *objectives* and overcome our *obstacles*. Plus, verbs free us from our concerns about line readings and listening to ourselves.

NOTE TO ACTORS: The "To be or not to be" exercise is about learning to play verbal and psychological *actions*. When rehearsing a scene, do not set the verbs prior to rehearsal but discover them while working with your acting partner. After you have finished working on a beat of a scene, stop. If a specific moment felt right, then try to figure out why it went well. Ask yourself, "What was I doing at that moment? What was the verb?" Then, pencil it in.

If at any time you are having a problem with a scene and don't know what to do, then study the script and think about possible verbs to try during your next rehearsal.

Verbs should come from the inside. You can only give—you can only play—what is happening to you internally. Therefore, verbs have to come from an inner, personal connection of cause and purpose that you have with the actor who is receiving the verb.

‹ EXERCISE 8: THE SHOE STORE ›

THIS EXERCISE TAKES PLACE is a shoe store. Two actors are selected to play the two characters: A clerk and a customer. During a big sale a week ago, the customer bought a pair of shoes. At the time of the sale, signage stated that all sales were final: no returns or exchanges. During the course of the week, the customer decides that they don't want the shoes but has lost the receipt. The customer's *objective* is to get a refund or exchange (the actor's choice). The clerk's *objective* is to enforce the store policy: no exchanges or refunds. It is important for the clerk not to pre-determine their verb. They will discover it spontaneously, depending on what verb they receive from the customer.

For this exercise, we need an empty shoe box. Actors should not open the box since there is nothing inside. A makeshift counter is set up with the clerk sitting behind it. It's a slow day at the shoe store, and the clerk's supervisor doesn't mind if the clerk reads while waiting for customers to arrive. (Actors should always have something to do. We are not waiting for the scene to start. Life is ongoing. *Acting is doing.*)

In this example, Dan plays the customer, and Nancy plays the clerk. Before beginning, I talk privately with Dan (the customer) and ask him what's wrong with the shoes?

DAN: They are the wrong size. I tried on a size 10, but these are a size 11.

ME: What is your *objective*?

DAN: I want an exchange.

ME: What verb are you going to play to achieve your *objective*?

DAN: To accuse.

ME: Okay, Dan. Be sure to land the verb immediately. Play it like you are playing a game of darts. Aim for the bull's-eye and avoid exposition.

Now that Dan has set up the given *circumstances*, it is important that he commits to and believes in these events.

The observing students are looking for two verbs: the customer's predetermined verb, and the clerk's spontaneously discovered verb, which is landed in response to the verb received from the customer.

For example, Dan (the customer) enters the store, approaches Nancy (the clerk), and slams the shoe box on the counter.

DAN
You sold me the wrong size shoes!

(*Nancy stands.*)

NANCY
Oh really. Let me see your receipt.

As soon as the two verbs are landed, I stop the scene and ask Nancy (the clerk) the following questions: "What did Dan (the customer) do to you? What verb did he play?" Then, I ask Dan (the customer) the same questions: "What did Nancy (the clerk) do to you? What verb did she play?"

Now, I encourage the class to join the discussion and weigh in regarding their observations about verbs. It is not important for the class to guess the exact verb. Any verb in the ballpark will do. For example, if the customer's verb was *to accuse*, then the class may come up with *to blame, to indict, to reproach*, etc. When I ask about the clerk's verb, the class might say *to question, to challenge, to interrogate, to control*, etc.

Furthermore, the class should pay attention to (and be aware of) everything that each actor has done to land their respective verb.

In our example with Dan and Nancy, perhaps the class talks about how Dan's physical choices—his brisk and determined walk prior to slamming the box on the counter—related to his verbal *action*: to accuse. These physical *actions* are notable since they happened before a word was even spoken. In fact, both actors were in *action* before a word was spoken.

Perhaps comment is made about Nancy's choice to stand and face Dan, which is another example of a physical choice that relates directly to her *action* and *objective*.

Each time actors work on this exercise, the choices they make become more creative. If actors continue to study with me from session to session, they will repeat this exercise many times.

For example, Ken, a professional actor who has studied with me off and on for several years and is usually cast in broad comedic roles, surprised me with one of his choices. When I asked him what *action* he was going to play, he said, "to scare." I thought to myself, "He's really going to go over the top on this one."

Instead, he calmly entered the shoe store and walked slowly to the clerk with his eyes focused on her. He quietly set the box on the counter, looked the clerk in the eyes, and slowly said (almost in a whisper), "I want my money back, now." The clerk retreated without a word, obviously playing the verb *to escape*. I stopped the exercise.

Both *actions* were landed, one without a word. Even though it is sometimes tempting, I try not to let the scene go beyond the first two verbs. It diverts the class away from the lesson of the exercise and instead focuses their energies on enjoying the scene.

Following the discussion, the process is reversed: the customer becomes the clerk, the clerk becomes the costumer, and the exercise is repeated. Everyone in class works this exercise. I stress to actors the importance of being aware of verbal, non-verbal, psychological, and physical *action* in their personal lives. Actors learn acting from life, and the choices actors make are what distinguish mediocre actors from extraordinary actors.

A book I have found very helpful as both a teacher and actor is *Actions: The Actors' Thesaurus* by Marina Caldarone and Maggie Lloyd-Williams. The book is a thesaurus of active verbs. Active verbs are powerful. If actors commit to and play *actions*, then the audience will suspend disbelief and accept the moment as true.

Verbs also stimulate the imagination. Equating active verbs to surreal images, Teju Cole wrote in the *New York Times*:

A main feature of surreal images is that they invite active verbs: they POUR and SHIMMER; they PUSH and SPRAY and BROOD, as though they had intentions. These kinds of images, in which the inanimate is suddenly animate, generate an open-ended visual conspiracy.

The same applies to acting. Suppose I go for a walk in a park and see one shoe—a perfectly good shoe—sitting at the trunk of a tree. I stop and think: "Why is that shoe at the bottom of the tree? How did it get here? What's its story?"

By endowing the shoe with a past (a backstory), the inanimate shoe becomes alive, and the viewer (or audience)—through incidence, *circumstance*, and *action*—begins to imagine the life of the shoe and its owner.

Therefore, I want actors to start thinking in terms of verbs. When actors play a verb, it is important for them to stay connected to their partner and observe how the verb landed. Did the verb work? Are they going to get what they want as a result of the verb? If not, then it might be a good idea to try a different verb.

◄ EVALUATION 4: FOURTH SIDE EXERCISE ►

IN SCENE WORK ELIZABETH has difficulty acknowledging the fourth side as part of her *place*. As a result, I have asked her to work on Uta Hagen's Fourth Side Exercise. Here, she presents it.

This exercise requires an actor to make or receive a phone call. While talking on the phone, the actor attempts to find moments in which their secondary focus can be placed on the fourth side of their environment—the area where the audience is sitting—while keeping their primary focus on the phone call (the *objective*). When working on the fourth side, actors should look in areas of the studio (or theatre) where they will not make eye contact with the audience.

Elizabeth's set is an office environment, complete with desk, chairs, laptop, phone, and papers. She picks up the phone, dials, and waits for her party to answer. While waiting, her eyes dart to the fourth side and then back to her papers. She doesn't use the fourth side again.

ELIZABETH
Hi, Jane? Elizabeth … I'm fine, thanks. Listen, there is a problem with your report.

Elizabeth continues on the call, explaining to Jane the technical problem and how to fix it. She then hangs up, looks at me, and says, "Scene."

ME: How did you feel?

ELIZABETH: The phone call felt good, but the fourth side didn't work. I felt self-conscious when I looked out there.

ME: The phone call was good. I believed you were talking and listening to Jane. How did the work on the fourth side feel in rehearsal?

ELIZABETH: Fine. And I did use it more in rehearsal.

ME: Of course. You had privacy because no one was watching you. Here, that is not the case, and you felt "self-conscious."

ELIZABETH: I know.

ME: What were you thinking about when you did use the fourth side?

ELIZABETH: I remembered I was supposed to look out there. I guess that's what I was thinking about.

ME: There is your problem. You have to be occupied with inner thoughts … or listening to Jane when you visually connect to the fourth side. In this case, while waiting for Jane to pick up, you might have been thinking about how to deal with her, or perhaps you could have been thinking about the great dinner you had with your boyfriend last night.

During the call, while listening to Jane, you could have used the fourth side. Instead, you looked at the papers on your desk. You could have had the same involvement while looking at the fourth side. You need to be involved in a thought process.

Before you started the exercise, I saw you set your points of focus on the fourth side. That process also should be a part of your scene setup. It is the right thing to do. The points you select need to be anchored on actual objects in the studio (or theatre) that you can safely focus on without making eye contact with the audience. What did you use here?

ELIZABETH: The center poster on the back wall.

ME: Good. You can imagine that poster to be anything you want. Make it something you are familiar with—like a family picture or hanging plant. When you look at it, you are not thinking that the picture needs to be straightened; you are thinking about how to handle Jane.

Elizabeth, rework this exercise for next week. Once you feel comfortable working with that aspect of *place*, you will want to incorporate the fourth side into everything you do.

When actors correctly use the fourth side, it opens up the scene, adds a fourth dimension to their *place*, and allows the audience to see the actors' eyes. Many actors pretend that the fourth side of their *place* doesn't exist. That's what Elizabeth does.

Human beings relate to all parts of their environment, and using the fourth side invites the audience directly into the space and into the actors' selves. Actors should not forget its importance.

◄ EVALUATION 5: *COLLECTED STORIES* (MONOLOGUE) ►

JEANNIE IS WORKING ON a monologue from *Collected Stories* by Donald Margulies. She has chosen the scene where Ruth tells Lisa about her first meeting with the poet, Delmar Schwartz.

Her set consists of a table and chair. She sits in the chair and presents the monologue.

ME: How did you feel?

JEANNIE: Pretty good. It took me awhile to get into it.

ME: Let's see ... where do I start?

(There is a groan from the class.)

ME: First, you started the monologue in the middle instead of at the beginning. Why?

JEANNIE: I was thinking of this as an audition piece. That's where the meat is.

ME: Right. Next week, start the monologue at the beginning, when you, as Ruth, arrive in New York—when you were in your early twenties. That way, you will discover how you reveal your *relationship* with Delmar.

You can still use the section you did today as an audition, but it will be much different. Today, you were here in the studio sitting at a table delivering the words. Where are you as Ruth?

JEANNIE: My apartment.

ME: How long have you lived here?

JEANNIE: Over thirty years.

ME: You need to work on *place*. Today, you were *placeless*. As you say, you have lived here a long time. This *place* is full of your stuff. Today, you were romanticizing the story. Read the play again. Ask yourself this question: "Who am I as Ruth?"

As a writer, Ruth has tried to keep romanticism and sentiment out of her work and life. Find that in you, Jeannie. Think about when you were in your early twenties, the people you knew, and the things you did. See if that helps you simply tell the facts—the events of the story. If that doesn't work, try this ...

Jeannie, you have been successful in business? Are you romantic and sentimental when negotiating a business deal?

JEANNIE: No. It is strictly business.

ME: Try tapping in to that part of you when you rework the monologue. Next class, please present it again for evaluation.

The next week, Jeannie brings in the monologue for rework. She sets up her apartment with a living room, a dining area, and a separate work area. It is obvious that she has been working on *place*. This time, she starts the monologue at the beginning. There is nowhere near the previous amount of sentiment and romanticism in her presentation. She is starting to find Ruth in herself.

ME: How did you feel today?

JEANNIE: Much better. The *place* helped a lot.

ME: It was better. You are now working in the right direction. The *place* gave you a privacy that wasn't there last week. I liked it when you went to the counter for the cookie. You were at home and beginning to find your Ruth. Keep going in that direction.

I liked what you wore today. The black slacks and top worked. You might want to rethink the color of the top. It is very lively. And your choice of shoes—the black leather boots with that heel—may not work for this monologue.

JEANNIE: Yes, I am beginning to see that. That's why I dressed down today. I need to be dowdy.

ME: Don't think dowdy. That seems negative. Think about what is comfortable for you, as Ruth. This will help. Since you have no plans to go out tonight, there is no occasion for you to dress.

There are two other points to consider. First, your *relationship* with your friend Elaine, and second, your physical description of Delmar. Regarding Elaine, you talk about her giving up her career as an actress. She gets married and dies of breast cancer at the age of thirty-nine. For you, as Ruth, what is the tragedy here? Why bring it up now?

JEANNIE: Well, she died of breast cancer at thirty-nine.

ME: Yes, that's terrible. We don't have control of when we die …
or what we die of. Those things happen.

JEANNIE: You mean the acting?

ME: Yes. From Ruth's point of view, she gave up her dream. The
playwright doesn't give us any more information than that.
There are just a few lines where you talk about Elaine. Then, she
is never mentioned again in the play. You, as Ruth, need to fill in
the backstory here.

    You were her friend and were probably at her wedding. Did
you approve of her marriage? In the monologue who are you
talking to?

JEANNIE: Lisa.

ME: Yes. Lisa is a talented grad student from your writing class at
Columbia. She has dreams of becoming a successful writer. She
is now becoming your friend, and you almost relate to her as the
daughter you never had. You are her mentor. Do you see what I
am getting at?

JEANNIE: I think so. It's a lesson?

ME: I don't think you are didactic. You are not hitting her over
the head with this. It is just a fact. The death from cancer is
horrible. The death of a dream is tragic. How many promising
young female students have you seen give up on their dreams?
Otherwise, why is it in the play? Work with this in rehearsal. See
what verbs are hiding under those words.

    Finally, we get to Delmar—the first time you see him and your
physical description of him. You worked hard at making him
repellent: the filth, the smell, and the yellow teeth. That became
more important than what followed. What is the next line in the
monologue?

JEANNIE: "There was something magnificent about him."

ME: Today, you almost threw that away. It became secondary to the description of his outer dissipation. You missed the most important part of your discovery.

JEANNIE: I wanted you guys to see him.

ME: You were thinking about the audience and not about what was important to Ruth. We will see him. Trust the playwright. You need to see his magnificence.

JEANNIE: I will work on these things. Stephanie and I are going to do a scene from this play.

ME: Good. What you learned from the monologue can be applied to the scene. It will help you. I look forward to seeing that.

◄ EVALUATION 6: *THE GLASS MENAGERIE* (MONOLOGUE) ►

JOHN IS WORKING ON the final narration from *The Glass Menagerie* by Tennessee Williams. He sits on a medium size stool and reads the narration.

ME: John, who are you talking to?

JOHN: The audience.

ME: It will help you if you give them an identity.

JOHN: I see what you mean. Well, I am in the Merchant Marines at this point. So, they could be some new friends that I have made there.

ME: That's a possibility. Try working with that. Use a *transfer* here. Find people—or it could be one person—that you personally know, and use that person—or persons—as your friends in the Merchant Marines, substituting them for the entire audience. Now, the audience becomes your acting partner.

This problem comes up in many plays—when the playwright asks actors to step out of the play and talk to the audience. When talking to the audience, you are still Tom, the character in the play, and you can either tell the story to a friend or a complete stranger. It is your choice. Both can work. If you do as I suggest, then you will discover the personal verbs that you need to play and develop a specific relationship with the audience.

You also have the problem of where to focus. If you are playing in a large theatre, then you can focus right over the heads of the audience. It will appear *as if* you are talking directly to them. Try talking to different sections of the audience. If you are playing in a small venue—one that seats no more than fifty—then you almost have to make eye contact with the audience. Don't stay connected to any one person for very long. Most people will get uncomfortable when an actor makes eye contact with them. It takes them out of the play.

John, you also have to come up with an *objective* for this narration. Why are you telling your friends this part of the story? What do you want?

Another acting problem you need to deal with is *place*. Where are you? In a theatrical performance, the actor playing Tom is usually in a lighting special during this monologue. In your mind, where are you? Consider what time it is. And consider what you are wearing.

Read the play again and study the narration. You will make more discoveries. For next week, bring in the first few beats, and we will talk more.

This monologue is a beautiful piece. It is poetry. Since this narration centers on your *relationship* with your sister Laura, it presents another problem for you. How long have you been away from Laura? Focus on this and the other issues I mentioned as we proceed with the narration. As you rehearse, focus on the problems we discussed.

◄ EVALUATION 7: *AN ENEMY OF THE PEOPLE* (MONOLOGUE) ►

DAN IS WORKING ON a monologue from *An Enemy of the People* by Henrik Ibsen, a play set in Norway during the 1880s. His character, Dr. Stockman, is a physician in a small town that has been developing a spa with the hope that it will draw tourists and be a financial boom for the community. Already, it is completely booked for the coming season.

As a precaution, Dr. Stockman has run some tests on the water and suspects there might be a problem. He sent the samples to a local university for further confirmation, and the results came back positive. He was right; the waters of the spa were contaminated.

In this monologue Dr. Stockman deals with revealing this information to his family and members of the press. His *objective* is to inform the citizens of the community and redo the spa project.

Dan's set consists of a table. He stands upstage from the table, holding a small piece of paper in his hands. He is having a problem with the words, gets stuck after the first couple of lines, and starts over. He stops and starts three different times. I can see he is blocked and suggest that he sit down and try it again later in the class.

At the end of class, I call on Dan to give it another try. He places himself in the same position on stage and starts the monologue. This time, he make it through the selected beats of the monologue.

ME: Dan, how did you feel?

DAN: I got through it. That was just the first couple of beats. I will have more for next week.

ME: You are starting off like you know that you are going to run into *obstacles*. You are playing the end of the play in the first scene. Try taking a positive approach. You, as Dr. Stockman, have discovered a good thing, and you expect the people to be grateful for your discovery. If you approach it from this perspective, then exciting discoveries will be in store for you.

The paper in your hands is important. It is the proof of your suspicions. You need to use it. Today, it looked like a piece of scrap paper. You rooted yourself to one spot—behind the table—and stayed there, which may be why you were having trouble with the words.

People from the press and your family are here. They are in different areas of the room. For the monologue, place them on different areas of the fourth side. You can move to them individually and make your points, which should help you overcome the problem of talking to a group of people. By approaching it this way, each person will have a different *relationship* to you and your discovery.

Also, pinpoint these *relationships*. They will activate you physically and psychologically. Depending upon whom you are dealing with, you will find different *actions*.

Dan has yet to rework this monologue. But he is back in class and working on an audition piece for a call back.

CHAPTER 6

~

CLASS FOUR: PHYSICAL ACTIONS

I N THIS CLASS STUDENTS present work on scenes, monologues, and exercises for evaluation. If time permits, we work on Exercise 10: Side Coached Actions. But first, we begin with a warm-up exercise.

‹ Exercise 9: Physical Actions ›

THIS EXERCISE IS A review and slight variation of Exercise Seven: To Be or Not To Be—which we worked on during the previous class— and is meant as a warm-up to focus the class.

To begin, I instruct the students to form a standing circle in the workspace. Using only Shakespeare's words (without verbs), we repeat the opening lines of Hamlet's soliloquy: "To be or not to be: that is the question." As the words move from actor to actor, they must be endowed with increasing speed and power, accelerating until they are traveling as fast as possible.

Next, we slow it down and add active verbs under Shakespeare's words. During this exercise, I ask the students to select the verbs.

In Class Three we verbally and psychologically explored the *actions* from a sitting position. In this class we are going to add— from a standing position—a physical dimension to each verb. Not only will actors look at their partners when playing each verb, they also will move to their partners and connect with them physically. For example, if the verb is *to organize*, then an actor might button their partner's shirt or fix their hair while physically, verbally, and psychologically *organizing* them.

Each verb must have cause, and actors need to know, personally, who they are organizing—and for what purpose. Actors should make these decisions prior to moving towards the selected receiving actors.

Suppose I imagine that Andrew, the actor I have selected to receive my verb, is my son. He is about to leave to pick up his prom date. This information is decided upon before I run to him, straighten his plaid shirt collar, and pat him on the back while saying my Shakespearian word: "To." Prior to my *actions*, I have internally connected to my son and the prom, focused on his shirt collar, and discovered my need *to organize* his appearance. This connection sends me into *action* and dictates exactly how I move towards my son.

After the giving actor delivers their verb, they change places with the receiving actor, who then selects a new actor and moves across the circle and delivers the verb (*to organize*)—with a different personalization and purpose—to the student they have selected. We use the same verb for the entire line of Shakespeare's dialogue. Then, a new verb is selected by an actor of my choice, and the exercise continues.

◄ EXERCISE 10: SIDE-COACHED ACTIONS ►

THIS EXERCISE TAKES PLACE in an employment office. Two actors are selected to play the two characters. One character is a new employee whose job at the office is to screen applicants (*objective*). This character has a tendency to feel sorry for the clients and has sent several unqualified applicants on job interviews. As a result, the company for which this character works has received some complaints, and the interviewer has been put on probation (*obstacle*). The other character is the applicant, who is looking for a job (*objective*). This person recently completed graduate school with a degree in aesthetics and has limited employment skills for the job market (*obstacle.*)

First, I instruct everyone in class to make a list of ten to fifteen active verbs. Then, each student reads their list aloud to ensure that only verbs—not adjectives, adverbs, or emotions—were written down. I also eliminate active verbs such as *to love, to hate, to cry, to laugh,* etc. that encourage actors to churn up emotions and force the emotional qualities of those verbs. It is important for actors to let emotion take them, rather than working directly for emotion.

Next, I select two more students and seat them in the front row. One student will side-coach the interviewer by giving them verbs to play from their list, and the other student will side-coach the applicant.

Side-coaches need to project their voices. The actors in the scene are involved in what is happening in the scene and need to be able to hear the provided verbs. If an actor can't hear a verb, then they have to stop the scene and ask the side-coach to repeat it, which interrupts the flow and the actors' involvement in the scene.

The scene starts with simple introductions and the applicant presenting their resume to the interviewer. Then, I signal one of the side-coaches by pointing to them. It doesn't matter which character gets the first verb.

For example, if I select the interviewer's side-coach to go first, then they will speak directly to the interviewer (played by Nancy), using the actor's first name: "Nancy, *to accuse.*" Once Nancy has time to play the verb and land it on her partner, then I cue the other side-coach, who will give the applicant (played by Kathy) a verb: "Kathy, *to confront.*"

Throughout the exercise, I continue to cue the side-coaches, alternating between interviewer and applicant. When one actor is given a new verb, the other actor should vocally back off their verb in order to give their partner an opportunity to play the new verb. For example, if Nancy is playing *to accuse* and a new verb (*to confront*) is given to Kathy, then Nancy continues to connect to her verb (*to accuse*) internally (non-verbally) until she is given a new verb, thus allowing Kathy to play her verb. If the actor cannot relate to a particular verb, then they can say, "Pass," and a new verb will be provided.

This exercise can be a lot of fun for the entire class. The side-coached verbs do not have to follow a logical progression, which helps animate the actors and assists them in finding the verbal, psychological, and physical dimensions of a single verb.

Since this exercise is not about thinking but about doing, it is important for actors to work on impulse. If actors stop to think about how to play a verb, then it is too late. That's why actors have the option to "pass."

Finally, this exercise provides actors with first hand practice in playing and landing verbs. In the scene actors are free to make bold and illogical choices while taking chances that result from the illogical verbs they are given to play. By committing to the verbs, actors can experience the real sensations that they strive to achieve in scene and monologue work. Hopefully, actors will start to think in terms of verbs when working on scenes and monologues.

During the exercise, I jot down the verbs that worked well and the verbs with which the actors had problems. Afterwards, we discuss my notes. Often, actors will realize a possible choice that they could have made, which is part of the learning process and something that should happen when rehearsing scenes, monologues, and exercises. Also, between rehearsals, actors should think of different choices to try in the next rehearsal.

◀ EVALUATION 8: CHANGES OF SELF EXERCISE (PART ONE) ▶

ALEK PRESENTS PART ONE of Uta Hagen's Changes of Self Exercise, which involves making or receiving three phone calls. He sets up a living room with couch, coffee table, magazines, and chairs and enters sipping on a straw protruding from a Styrofoam cup. After sitting down on the couch and placing his cup on the coffee table, Alek removes his cell phone from his pocket and places it on the table next to the cup. He tries to find a comfortable position in which to take a nap. Soon, he falls asleep.

After a moment, the phone rings, and Alek wakes to answer it.

ALEK

Oh, hi Mom. No, I'm fine. Listen, thank you so much. That really helped out. I was able to buy some decent food for a change. It was a surprise. And thank you again … The band is great. We are performing tonight at nine. I would love for you to come … Great! I will look for you. See you tonight … Love you too.

He hangs up the phone and lies back down. The phone rings again.

ALEK

What's up David? No, David. The performance is tonight at nine. Yes, I am sure. No, David. It is not this afternoon at three. It is at nine o'clock tonight. Got it? What time is the performance, David? … Right! I will see you then … No, David. You did not leave your guitar here. David, I want you to think. When was last time you had your guitar? Well, you probably left it at Jen's then. Go over to her apartment and see if it is there. David, I have to take another call. I will see you at nine tonight.

Alek clicks over and takes the incoming call.

ALEK

What is it, Dad? Yes, she did help me. She is always there for me, not like you. Dad, don't start this again. For the last time, I am not going back to college. I need to take this time off. You can't tell me what to do … I am doing something … Yes, the band … and it is important to me. Dad? Dad?

Alek hangs up the phone, looks at me, and says, "Scene."

ME: Alek, how did you feel?

ALEK: Pretty good.

ME: It was good. First, your entrance worked. You had a good sense of destination. Next time you work for destination, try working without a prop. Find an appropriate physical *action* related to where you are coming from and execute it off stage just before entering. Your fourth side work was excellent when you were on the phone. It is great that you incorporated the acting problems from the first two exercises into this one.

The three calls presented three different parts of you. The first one to Mom: the warmth, caring, and ease that exists between the two of you was apparent; you are friends. Second, David: you are his caretaker. It was like you were the parent and he was the child. Third, Dad: a difficult *relationship* for both of you. You are rebelling against his authority. We saw the assertive side of you. You tried to make him feel guilty.

All three worked. We saw three different parts of you. Depending upon your *relationship* with each of the three people you talked to, your *objective* changed. I particularly liked the Dad conversation. I saw your pain and vulnerability—and your attempt to cover them. In the course of about two minutes, we saw your behavior change dramatically. This exercise is a great way for actors to discover the many different behaviors of the self. It opens the door for actors to play many different characters that originate from the sense of self.

In this case, Alek, we saw who you are when talking to Mom, David, and Dad. Each one was different. But there was one aspect of the work that wasn't complete. Do you know what it was?

ALEK: I am not sure ... the sleep?

ME: Yes. You were anticipating the phone call. The first part of lying down and trying to find the right sleep position was good. When you close your eyes in the sleep position, let your mind go to something outside this *place*. For example, visualize yourself in a field of clover, or picture yourself sitting on a beach, watching a crashing wave. Then, when the phone rings, you will have to pull yourself away from that *place* and return to the apartment and the phone call. If you do that, then the sleep will work for you. Good work, Alek.

We have all seen actors, especially in films and on television, play variations of the same character, over and over again. They have found something that works for them commercially and are playing only that singular image of themselves. As a result, agents, producers, directors, and writers think only of that image. After a few years, these actors stop working, and we ask, "Whatever happened to so and so?" Unfortunately, they have outlived that one-dimensional image, and the audience has tired of seeing it.

Two actors who have not fallen into this trap come to mind: Meryl Streep and Tom Hanks, who both started and trained in theatre. In every film in which they appear, each presents different parts of self that are used in creating the characters they play.

Wesley Morris, critic-at-large for the *New York Times* commented on this ability to create characters from the self:

> What is it about watching someone become someone else that has been so mesmerizing ...? What is it about a person's becoming his or her ultimate self that we can't resist? It is all powerful, all consuming stuff. In life that can be dangerous. But in art, I want my mind controlled by that power. I want an actor's skill, intelligence, energy, body and face to overtake me.

Therefore, the Changes of Self Exercise is an excellent example of how actors can discover the many different behaviors in ourselves that allow us to play a multitude of characters. This exercise can be repeated many times.

◄ EVALUATION 9: *PROOF* (SCENE) ►

HALEY AND ELISE ARE presenting a scene from *Proof* by David Auburn. In this scene between Claire and Catherine, the two sisters engage in passionate dialogue. Their father, Robert, was a brilliant mathematician at the University of Chicago but was plagued by mental illness, enjoying only occasional periods of lucidity. Catherine seems to have inherited his gift and possibly his illness.

Claire, the older sister, is also accomplished in the field of mathematics but lacks the creative genius of her father and younger sister. She has a successful career in finance and has been living in New York with her live-in boyfriend, who has "connections." Claire has returned to Chicago to attend her father's funeral, to settle the affairs of the home, and to look after Catherine.

She suspects that Catherine is mentally unstable, and against Catherine's will, she has put the family home on the market and pressured Catherine to move to New York. The scene starts as the two sisters eat breakfast on the porch of the old house, only hours before their flight to New York.

ME: How did you feel?

ELISE: Good.

HALEY: I felt good, too. I thought we made good connections to each other.

ME: You should feel good. You solved a number acting problems in the scene. Haley, your entrance worked. You established destination—coming from inside the house after you finished packing.

You both had a very good handle on your *relationship* and who you are in the play. Your connections were good. I am glad you chose this scene. It has different levels to it. In other scenes between Katherine and Claire, the conflicts were overtly expressed. In this scene you are both attempting to cover the conflicts. You found the awkwardness and discomfort in the encounter.

Elise, the difficulty you had in your attempt to make everything pleasant and encouraging about the move was the right choice. You were trying to justify your decisions about the house and Catherine. We saw you covering your inner feelings of self-doubt and possible guilt.

Haley, we saw your attempt to go along with Elise and get through this ordeal as painlessly as possible. We also saw you covering your inner feelings of betrayal as well as your insecurities and anxieties. Both of your *objectives* were clear.

You both also worked well with the objects in the scene, balancing the outer behavior with the inner objects. You created tension in the scene. We could see that it was difficult for the two of you to communicate.

You had a good start on *place*. This whole play takes place outdoors, on the porch. Outdoor behavior is different than indoor behavior. You made some general attempts in that direction, but you need to be more specific. I saw you both working for temperature. It is early fall, and there is a chill in the air—as well as in the *relationship*. In the rework find specifically on your bodies where you are physically aware of this chilly air and what you do about it.

Visually, you need to see the landscapes around you. When we are outdoors, our vision is expanded. Since there are no walls blocking our view, we can see much further. Put things out there, in that space, that you are familiar with, such as trees, the house next door, the skyline, plants in the yard, etc.

This is your family home, and this is the last time you will see these things. You are not only making visual connections but also emotional ones.

You both should feel good about the work you are already doing. Next time, try creating four forth-sides around you, where all four of the fourth-sides are primary. Find points of focus here in the studio, and place your objects just like you did in the Fourth Side Exercise. Let's give this scene one more week, focusing on outdoors and *place*.

Haley had to drop the class before the rework could be presented.

◄ **EVALUATION 10:** *PAINTING CHURCHES* (**MONOLOGUE**) ►

JAN IS WORKING ON a monologue from *Painting Churches* by Tina Howe. Her character, Fanny, is recalling experiences from when she was much younger. After heavy snows fell in Boston, she and her poet husband, Garr, would bundle up and ride a single sled down Beacon Hill onto the Boston Common.

Now in their late seventies, the couple—as a result of Garr's dementia—has found it necessary to downsize and move from their spacious Beacon Hill residence to their small beach cottage on Cape Cod. As Fanny sorts through their old belongings, deciding what to keep and what to toss, she discovers a pair of Garr's old rubber boots, complete with metal fasteners to keep out the snow. The boots serve as the springboard for her recollection of the sledding experience, which happened before their only child, Maggs, who is now a successful portrait artist, was born. Fanny likens the sledding adventures to sex rituals.

Jan (as Fanny) sits on the couch, still in the clothes she wore to class: an attractive sweater and dark slacks. She places a pair of leather boots by her feet and endows them *as if* they are the rubber boots. In this monologue Fanny is talking to Mags (her daughter), who Jan has placed on the fourth side of the room.

Jan picks up one of the boots and starts the monologue. She has put a lot of work into the text and, on one level, understands her *objective*, with which she has found identification.

ME: Jan, how did you feel?

JAN: I felt pretty good, I think.

ME: You have put in a lot of work on this. I want you to rework it for next week.
    Here's what I want you to work on ... First, what are you wearing as Fanny? How is Fanny dressed?

JAN: In the play? I am wearing an old bathrobe, pajamas, slippers, and an old hat from a thrift store.

ME: Right. See if you can come up with those clothes. See how they influence your behavior. Second, what other things are in the room with you?

JAN: Boxes of stuff that I am sorting through.

ME: You need to work with those things as well. Out of that activity, you discover the boots. That didn't happen today.

JAN: I can do that.

ME: One more thing you need to consider: how is your *relationship* with your daughter?

JAN: On the surface, it is all right. She is an only child, and I love her. I am thinking that she was an unexpected child. She is Garr's girl—always was and still is.

In the first scene when Mags arrives from New York, I am stuck in a dress. It's over my head, and I can't get it on or off. But they pay me no mind. It's all hugs and kisses and talk of her trip as I am struggling with the dress. I felt—and feel—left out.

ME: When did the sledding stop?

JAN: When Mags was born.

ME: Does that add another level to your *objective*?

JAN: It could. I will think about it.

ME: See if it colors the *objective*. When you did the monologue today, it was a memory from the past, and it stayed there. It was sentimental. See if, in the rework, you can bring the memory into the present—with a purpose that relates to your daughter. I look forward to seeing it next week.

For the rework, Jan sets up the room with added boxes of old possessions. She changes into pajamas, bathrobe, slippers, and an old wicker hat. As a result of a focus on wardrobe and *place*, the monologue is completely different. This time it takes place in the present tense, right in this room with her daughter.

ME: How did you feel today?

JAN: So much better. The clothes and boxes helped so much. I did discover the boots.

ME: Yes you did.

JAN: I see what you mean about Mags. I wanted her to know about our lives when we were young—and how close we were and still are. I wanted to share that *relationship* with her. I lost some of that after Mags was born. Also, Mags doesn't want to accept what is happening to Garr's mind.

ME: That took the scene from a sentimental memory of the past to something that was happening in this room today. Excellent work, Jan. Any questions?

JAN: I don't think so. Thank you.

CHAPTER 7

~

CLASS FIVE: CHARACTER AS SELF

I N THIS CLASS STUDENTS present work on scenes, monologues, and exercises for evaluation. If time permits, we work on Exercise 12: The Waiting Room. But first, we begin with a warm-up exercise.

◄ EXERCISE 11: ADDING ►

I INSTRUCT THE STUDENTS to form a sitting circle in the workspace. Each student is assigned a number, starting with "1" and following in consecutive order (2, 3, 4, etc.).

In this exercise, the students send numbers to each other instead of the words "To be or not to be." It's quite simple: Student A sends their number to Student B. Then, Student B sends their number to Student C, who adds the two numbers and sends that sum to Student D. The sequence repeats.

Students always send their own number to the actor of their choice, unless they are the third person in the sequence, in which case they send the sum of the two previous numbers. Then, we start all over, with the fourth and fifth students sending their own numbers and the sixth student adding the previous two numbers.

For example, let's suppose I assign 1 to Nancy, 2 to Kathy, 3 to Dan, 4 to Mary, 5 to Frank, and 6 to Ellen. The exercise begins when Nancy looks at the student of her choice (in this case Mary) and says, "One," verbally sending her number to Mary. Next, Mary looks at the student of her choice (in this case Dan) and says, "Four," verbally sending her number to Dan. Now, Dan, since he is the third student in the sequence, instead of sending his own number (3) to the student of his choice (in this case Kathy), adds together the previous two numbers (1 and 4) and says "Five," verbally sending the sum to Kathy. The sequence continues, with Kathy sending her number (2) to another student, that student sending their own number to a third person who then adds the previous two numbers.

As the exercise continues and a rhythm is discovered, the pace increases: boom boom, add; boom boom, add. If the ensemble moves too slow, then their minds shut down. But if they keep up the pace, then a rhythm can be established.

This exercise is not a lesson in mathematics. If someone makes a mistake adding, we keep going. What's important is that actors know when to add and that their focus is where it needs to be.

This exercise is about staying in the moment—about keeping the acting instrument alive in the present tense. Actors should not think ahead or behind but keep their focus in the present moment.

Common missteps that happen to actors in a performance are thinking about the horrible mistake they made in the last beat (or how wonderful they were in the last moment) or thinking ahead to the emotional climax of the scene that occurs in the next beat. This exercise helps actors stay focused on the present moment.

◄ EXERCISE 12: THE WAITING ROOM ►

IF TIME PERMITS AFTER the presentation and evaluation of scenes, monologues, and exercises, the class works on this exercise, which takes place in a hospital waiting room equipped with couch, chairs, coffee table, magazines, and check-in table with a blank piece of paper and a pen on it.

For this exercise, I select no more than four actors at time. Each participant has arrived at the hospital waiting room to pick up and drive home a friend or family member following a minor outpatient procedure.

A sign in the waiting room states that the receptionist has been called away and asks visitors to sign-in with the name of the patient they are waiting for and the current time.

Next, I speak privately with the three or four selected actors, one at a time, and remind each of the importance of knowing who they have come to pick up and what medical procedure was performed on that person.

Finally, I provide each actor with one characteristic: timid, aggressive, compulsive, selfish, optimistic, etc. All of these characteristics exist within each one of us and can be released through *action*.

Usually, the characteristic I assign is different from the self-image presented by the actor. For example, if the actor presents a self-image of open and outgoing, then I might give the characteristic of frightened or insecure. I want actors to discover different behaviors in themselves, which will allow them to bring greater dimension to their work while opening the door for the variety and number of characters they can play.

To start the exercise, I call the actors into the waiting room one at a time and encourage them to enter with personal belongings, such as coats, packages, briefcases, pocketbooks, cell phones, etc. These items give actors objects with which to work and, consequently, provide them with more things to do.

Actors, however, should enter the waiting room as their neutral selves—not thinking about their assigned characteristic—and forget their preconceived images of how a timid or aggressive person might act, which is often the first thing most actors go for based upon what they have learned from watching films and television. I want actors to see if they can find in them (and then release) the assigned characteristic through *actions* (verbs) with the objects and people they come into contact with in the waiting room. Remember, the people in the waiting room are strangers.

Think about how many times we have been thrown into an unexpected situation and found ourselves behaving in a way that we never dreamed we were capable of behaving. Even though many people have a limited understanding of who they are as humans, each person possesses the potential to behave in myriad ways.

While watching this exercise, I pay close attention to each actor's entrance. If an actor enters with an attitude relating to the assigned characteristic, they have started on the wrong foot. It is not uncommon when an actor works on this exercise for the first time.

If an actor is exploring their ideas and images of an aggressive person and not exploring it personally through verbal, non-verbal, physical, and psychological *action*, then the ideas and images will result in general behavior rather than specific personal behavior. Illustrating a character will lead to that character becoming a caricature.

I purposely have given the actors their first two *actions*: *to read* the waiting room sign and to *sign-in*. Depending on the choices actors make when executing these two *actions*, much information about a character can be revealed.

After all the actors have entered the waiting room and had an opportunity to explore the exercise, I stop work and ask the observing students two questions: Who are these people? What did they do to reveal themselves?

For example, Mary's characteristic is "meticulous." She is the first to enter and comes in as herself. After entering, Mary observes the room, spots the sign, studies it, and picks up the pen. Instead of using it, she sets it back down on the table, opens her purse, takes out her own pen, and signs the check-in sheet, first printing her name before beautifully drawing her signature.

Next, Mary finds a chair in which to sit. She removes a tissue from her purse and wipes the chair. Satisfied, Mary folds the tissue and drops it into the waste basket across the room. She then returns to her chair and sits down with both feet planted firmly on the floor. Now, Mary notices the magazines on the coffee table, picks them up, and arranges them by publication date before setting them back down on the table in a neat pile. At this point, I cue another actor to enter.

If verbal interaction occurs between Mary and the other actors, then her choices of verbal and psychological *action* should reflect her given characteristic: meticulous.

While working on this exercise for many years, I have noticed huge transformations in some actors, including their physical bodies being redefined and their vocal instruments taking on new colors and pitches. As a result of this exercise, some actors are able to think differently and deal with new inner objects (thoughts.) By abandoning the image of themselves that they present in every day life, these actors are able to look and sound like different people. In essence, they have found a new persona inside themselves

Sometimes, instead of providing actors with a characteristic, I will give them a verb. For example, I might give a shy student the verb *to pontificate*. When exploring this exercise for the first time, verbs are often easier to work with than characteristics. The preferred method, however, is to assign a characteristic since directors often provide actors with a characteristic note, which is used to bring out what is needed in the play. It is then up to actors— by playing multiple *actions*—to translate and release characteristics into personal, playable doings.

NOTE TO ACTORS AND TEACHERS: Once, I was asked to play Reverend Fred Phelps in a new play, *The Visions of Right* by Marcia Cabulska. Phelps—an intolerant minister from Topeka, Kansas— preached hatred of homosexuals. He (and his family, including young children) picketed any event that dealt with gay issues. In fact, they picketed a performance of this play in Topeka, carrying signs that said, "GOD HATES FAGS." The Phelps family also picketed a production of *The Laramie Project* that I directed at Rockhurst University in Kansas City. They even picketed the funerals of soldiers killed in action in Afghanistan and Iraq, hatefully protesting the military for abandoning "don't ask don't tell" and the government for sanctioning homosexuality via same-sex marriage.

As a gay man, playing Phelps was indeed a challenge. My first thought was, "I am nothing like Fred Phelps. I am an introvert and a liberal democrat who believes in total equality and freedom for all people. I am a fighter for just causes." That fact was something that Phelps and I had in common: we are both fighters. Otherwise, we are worlds apart.

Additionally, I despise bullies. Reverend Phelps was a bully. So, just as in the Waiting Room Exercise, I worked with the characteristic of *a bully*. Also, *to bully* is a great verb, and it proved to be a key *action* for me. I was able to *transfer* my hatred of bullies onto the Phelps character, which aided me in finding the passion to preach the rhetoric that spewed from me as the minister. I felt it important for the performance to make a statement disavowing the evil that Phelps preached and his persecution of others. When viewing the character (and my approach) through this lens, I became excited to take on the challenge of playing Phelps. It is amazing what we can find in ourselves.

◄ EVALUATION 11: *DINNER WITH FRIENDS* (SCENE) ►

DAN AND MARY ARE reworking Act One, Scene Two from *Dinner with Friends* by Donald Margulies. They are playing Tom and Beth, who have been married for ten years and have a four year old son, Sam. Tom is having an affair with another woman and is living away from home. A snow storm stranded him at the airport and forced him to come back to the house for the night. Beth has been at a dinner party hosted by their longtime friends, Karen and Gabe. Much of the scene deals with Tom questioning Beth about what happened at dinner. He is trying to find out if Beth told their friends about the affair and separation.

In the first presentation of the scene, *place*, *objectives*, and their *relationship* to each other worked well, but I felt that their important *relationship* with Karen and Gabe was too general.

Since the title of the play is *Dinner with Friends*, I asked Dan and Mary to define specifically the title of the play and the events of the dinner party. Even though Dan (as Tom) was not in attendance for this party, he has been to many dinner parties at the home of Karen and Gabe and should be able to visualize those events.

I also asked Dan and Mary to read the play again, focus on their *relationship* with Karen and Gabe, and find a personal *transfer* for them. Each actor should do this individually as homework by finding different people in their life experience that could be used as *transfers* for Karen and Gabe. The *transfers*, of course, will be different for both actors but will serve the play. If the *transfers* work, then Dan and Mary will discover new *actions* relating to Karen and Gabe, and there will be a personal history between the characters. (See Class Six for a more specific discussion about *transfers*.)

For example, if my *relationship* with Karen and Gabe is similar to my *relationship* with real life friends Jill and Jack, then my behavior with Jill and Jack will be the same as—or similar to—my behavior with Karen and Gabe. Therefore, Dan and Mary must tap into their personal lives in order to find their specific on stage *relationships* with Karen and Gabe. They should not try to impose the physical image of their *transfers* onto the actors playing Karen and Gabe. Trying to do so will drive them crazy.

When the reworked scene is finished, I ask Dan and Mary how they felt. They both said that they felt good.

DAN: Yeah, the *transfers* really helped. I could feel the difference. I knew who I was talking about.

ME: Yes, I could see that. The *transfers* led you to specific *actions*.

MARY: Mine did too. In fact, I was at my *transfers* for dinner last night.

ME: Don't say another word. Keep your *transfers* private, otherwise you will ruin them for yourself. You both should feel good. The *transfers* worked. This time, there was a history in the *relationships*. The work was specific. You were living in the *place*—in the present tense. Good work. Decide what you want to work on next. If you need help, let me know.

◀ EVALUATION 12: *THE GLASS MENAGERIE* (MONOLOGUE) ▶

ELLEN IS WORKING ON—as a monologue—the confrontation scene between Amanda and Laura in *The Glass Menagerie* by Tennessee

Williams. In this scene Amanda has just returned from a visit to Rubicon's Business School where she enrolled Laura, hoping that Laura would find a career as a secretary. Amanda has learned from the typing teacher that Laura has not been attending class. The stress was too much for her; it made her sick to her stomach.

> ME: Ellen, you have a good understanding of the *objective* and a fragmented sense of *place*—just a coat tree, a couch, and a small table for the menagerie. You also seemed vague about where Laura was physically. Where is Laura?

> ELLEN: She just ran to her typing table to pretend she was practicing.

> ME: Where is that here—in your space? You need a specific point of focus on the fourth side.

> ELLEN: Right. I was visualizing it in my head, but I didn't anchor it here physically.

> ME: Right, Ellen. For next week, work on that: the fourth side.
>   You also need a picture of Laura's father, who deserted the family. Somewhere in the room, you probably want to simulate a phonograph. It is another safe haven for Laura, a *place* where she can escape to.
>   And you don't have anything in here that belongs to Tom. You might want to include something of his. On your entrance, you eliminated the first line. Why did you do that?

> ELLEN: I didn't know what to do with the "deceptions."

> ME: Many actors have had problems with that line. See if you can organically justify the use of the three words: "Deception, deception, deception!" Think about your life as Amanda and the different experiences you have had—and the times where you have been deceived. Think about your most immediate experience with deception.

ELLEN: I will try.

ME: Something else that needs to be considered in this scene is *expectation*. This is important. Amanda was *expecting* to be inducted as an officer in the DAR. This is a big event for you. For what office have you been elected? Williams doesn't tell us. You need to make that specific. This position is a sign of acceptance and approval by your peers. It is very important to you. You planned and dressed for this event. In fact, the dress you are wearing today should be a reminder of your *expectations*.

Before going to the DAR, you stop off at the business school to check on the progress of your daughter. You were *expecting* good results. After meeting with Laura's teacher and receiving the bad news, you never made it to the DAR. Next week, see how these events and your *expectations* influence your entrance. Your *expectations* are unspoken thoughts and affect your inner and outer behavior.

For the rework, Ellen sets up the *place* by adding the picture of the father, a phonograph, and a book on the table. She enters and starts to take off her coat. Her eye catches the menagerie and Laura, who is moving to the typing table, which she has specifically placed on the fourth side. Ellen goes for the "deceptions," but they don't work. She is pushing for them and trying to make them meaningful by shouting. The rest of the scene, however, works well.

ME: Ellen, how did you feel?

ELLEN: The "deceptions" didn't work.

ME: No, they didn't. You were forcing them. You were working too hard. Internally, as Amanda, you are dealing with massive pain and disappointment. You notice Laura hurrying to the typing table, and you verbalize, "Deception, deception, deception!" Out of these events and the inner thoughts you are dealing with, try to find a verb. Today, you were yelling, and it wasn't coming from any specific place. Ellen, it has to come from inside—inner thoughts you connect to that relate to the fact that you have been deceived. Out of those thoughts, an *action* should come, an active verb.

ELLEN: How about *to resign* myself? This is my fate.

ME: That's a possibility. I don't think you are ready to give up. I think the deceptions might have to do with Laura and your discoveries about her today. Try playing the verb *to resign* and see what happens. You might find other verbs that will work for you.

The rest of the scene went very well. You should feel good. You did a good job containing your anger, putting a lid on it. There were occasional outbursts that were right for the scene. You tried to control yourself. I liked it when you picked up Tom's book and slammed it back down. We saw your pain and frustration. As Amanda, you don't know where to go from here. You are at an emotional bottom. Your *expectations* have turned to failures.

Ellen, you have found many colors in this monologue—from pain, disappointment, anger, desperation, and love. If you had a real Laura to work with, you would have made many more discoveries. At one point, you walked over to the menagerie and picked up one of the glass animals. You looked at it, and it seemed *as if* you wanted to crush it. You then set it back on the table. That was a wonderful choice. Lots of good work here. Ellen. You should feel good.

ELLEN: I do.

◄ EVALUATION 13: SHAKESPEARE'S SONNET 130 ►

COOPER IS PRESENTING SONNET 130 by William Shakespeare. He has been working on this piece for an audition. The sonnet pokes fun at poets who have compared the beauty of their mistresses to flowers, the sun, snow, perfume, etc.

Cooper had a good start until the last two lines, when he blanked and forgot the words. He tried it a second time with the same result. I asked him to sit down and told him that we would try it again at the end of class. Unfortunately, the third time did not work either. He still could not remember the last two lines.

Finally, someone in class Googled the sonnet and came up with the last two lines: "And yet, by heaven, I think my love as rare/As any she belied with false compare."

Those final two lines are the button on the sonnet, and they express Shakespeare's entire point: an attempt to poke fun at poets who use overly romantic metaphors. In these lines Shakespeare is comparing the down-to-earth attributes of his mistress to the fanciful qualities of other Elizabethan poets. Cooper struggled because the word "belied" was giving him trouble.

ME: Did you look up "belied" in the dictionary?

COOPER: Well, I know what it means. It's just the obscure structure.

The dictionary defines belied as "to picture falsely, to misrepresent, to show to be false."

ME: Look it up, and I think it will clarify the meaning of those lines. You will discover strong *actions* for those lines. If you do that, then you will have a good audition piece.

Cooper, where are you? What environment are you in?

COOPER: I'm in a tavern.

ME: You know in your head that you are in a tavern, but you are not doing anything about it.

At the audition, you will have a chair—use it. Get a chair from the back.

Cooper grabs a chair and stands behind it, with his hands on top of the chair.

ME: There, you can use it like that. You can put one foot on the seat of the chair, or you can sit down. Whatever you decide, it will occupy you physically. It will relax you, and your physical tension will disappear since you are doing something about the tavern.

◄ EVALUATION 14: *RABBIT HOLE* (MONOLOGUE) ►

TANGELA IS WORKING ON a monologue from *Rabbit Hole* by David Lindsay-Abaire. Her *objective* is to convince her husband that she is not trying to erase the memory of their four year old son, Danny, who was accidentally killed when he ran in front of a car while chasing his dog.

ME: How did you feel?

TANGELA: Too emotional?

ME: Yes. You were working too hard to find the emotion. An actor will read this scene and say, "This is really emotional." The actor will then work to churn up that emotion. This is exactly what you did.

I want to go back and talk about the first exercise you did, the Destination Exercise. You are a nurse, and you took something from a real life experience that you had. Am I correct?

TANGELA: Yes.

ME: You set up a crib-like structure and put a life size baby doll in it. Then, you made an entrance from another part of the hospital and went to the crib, took down some pictures that had been taped to the side of it, put them in an envelope, and placed the envelope on a table. You endowed the doll to be a child as you removed and disposed of the diaper and cleaned her. It soon was apparent that the child had died. Finally, you received a call asking you to go to another department. As you spoke on the phone, you fought to control your emotions.

Tangela, that fight to control your emotions was missing from your work today. You need to fight the emotion and try to stay in control, as you did in the hospital. It's what we do in life. As Ms. Hagen would say, "We fight for normalcy." When you work this way, emotion usually increases since we always lose the battle.

This is a good role for you, Tangela. If you want to work on it again, then focus on this area. I know your schedule will not allow you to attend the next session of classes, but don't give up on it.

CHAPTER 8

~

CLASS SIX: TRANSFERENCE

IN THIS FINAL CLASS of our six-week session, students present work on scenes, monologues, and exercises for evaluation and possible rework (if they plan on taking the next term). We also have a broader discussion about *transference*, including work on an exercise that specifically deals with the use of *self-transference*. But first, we begin with a warm-up exercise.

◄ EXERCISE 13: WAITING WITH A CONDITION ►

THIS EXERCISE, WAITING WITH a Condition, incorporates elements from Uta Hagen's sixth and seventh exercises: Bringing the Outdoors on Stage and Finding Occupation While Waiting.

First, I select three or four actors. Each actor is waiting outside for a specific person (a friend, relative, acquaintance, etc.) who will take them to a specific event (a movie, a play, dinner, etc.). The actors fill in the exact details: who they are waiting for and what event they are going to. The outdoor *place* of the meeting has been agreed upon by both parties.

The actors have arrived at the right *place* at the right time, but the person they are waiting for is late. Weather conditions and temperature, which will be different for each actor, need to be considered. Even though the actors physically occupy the same workspace, each actor needs to block out the other actors and visualize the space as their own. For example, one actor might be standing in front of Barnes & Noble at a shopping mall on a fall afternoon, and another actor might be waiting at the entrance to a city park on an early morning in May.

While waiting, the actors need to work with inner objects (thoughts). These inner thoughts can, of course, jump around—from an unpaid bill to a movie, an upcoming dinner party, or an argument with a boss. It's the way that we think. For this exercise, it is no different. There should be no outward logical order to the thinking.

Physical occupation should exist as well. Actors might look in the direction from where their person is coming, shift their weight, walk on a crack in the sidewalk, adjust physically to the weather, etc.

While actors are waiting, they also must deal with a specific condition, which can be the cold, the heat, a headache, back pain, an itch, etc. Each actor chooses the condition that affects their behavior. It should be a minor irritation and not a debilitating condition. Nor should it be a condition from which actors are currently suffering.

When working with this condition, actors should first isolate the specific location on their bodies where they are most sensitive to it. If my condition is *a headache*, then it might exist on my forehead, right between my eyes. As a result, I place my focus and concentration on that part of my body and imagine the pressure.

Next, actors must decide what to do about the condition, which does not have to be logical. For example, to deal with my headache, I may close my eyes, massage the spot where it hurts, rotate my head, etc.

In some instances, the condition will travel. If the condition is *being cold*, then I might start with the feeling in my toes. What do I do about it? I curl up my toes. If the cold feeling spreads to the back of my neck or the tips of my fingers, then I would discover additional *actions* (or doings).

This exercise contains many acting problems, which actors should work on only one at a time, e.g., actors can move from checking their watch to dealing with a headache to worrying about an unpaid bill. Actors should not attempt to work on all the problems simultaneously.

Furthermore, actors should not worry about trying to illustrate their condition to the audience. Actors must, instead, focus on their abilities to believe in, through concentration and doing, the reality of their conditions. If they work this way, then the physical problem will communicate itself.

Finally, this exercise is about imagination, concentration, sense memory, and *action-doing*. It is not about waiting to feel. Actors can wait forever to feel and nothing will happen.

There are numerous plays where characters deal with a condition (or conditions): alcoholism, drug addiction, chronic pains, etc. Often, actors who are working on characters that suffer from a condition will illustrate the condition rather than creating its reality through specific focus and doing.

Once the actors in the workspace have had enough time to explore all of the problems, I stop the exercise and ask each actor what physical condition they were exploring and if they felt that it worked. Following the discussion, the remaining actors in class will repeat this exercise in the same manner.

NOTE TO ACTORS AND TEACHERS: Work on the Hagen exercises has paid off for me personally. In 2005 I played Morrie Schwartz in *Tuesdays with Morrie* by Mitch Albom. Morrie suffers from amyotrophic lateral sclerosis (ALS), a degenerative disease also known as Lou Gehrig's disease. During the course of the play, Morrie's condition changes from normal mobility to a cane, a walker, a wheelchair, a recliner, and then a bed.

At one point in the play, I (as Morrie) am sitting at a table writing in my journal and need a book—which contains a quote from the poem "O Tell Me the Truth About Love" by W.H Auden—from the bookcase. It is my singular focus, and I am not thinking about anything else. For a brief moment, I forget about my disability, stand up, and take one step towards the bookcase. The muscles in my right leg fail and lock up. As I reach for the cane, it falls to the floor. I lose my balance and pitch forward, grabbing the back of a dining room chair to try to keep from falling. It topples, and I break the fall with my right arm.

As an actor, I know when this moment is coming up in the scene. Before I stand, my inner and outer focus must be on the poem and making it to the bookcase to retrieve the book. In order to make the upcoming fall believable, I have to divert my attention away from it. If I don't do this, then I will anticipate the fall, and it will appear false. The moment needs to come across *as if* it were unplanned.

In order to make this fall physically work for me, I chose a *condition*: my right leg had fallen asleep. Under this condition, my right leg would not be able to support me. Reaching for the cane and chair are my *actions*. I am in full control of the fall as I attempt to reach my destination: the bookcase. It should appear to the audience that Morrie is not in control.

◄ EXERCISE 14: USE OF SELF-TRANSFERENCE ►

IN THE WORKSPACE STUDENTS set up, as best they can, a multipurpose store by gathering items from our prop storage and refreshment areas and placing them on makeshift counters (stools and tables work nicely). If there is a shopping cart in the studio, then it would be great prop to use in this exercise. I rescued one that had been abandoned in our front yard, and now, it resides in our prop area.

This exercise requires two actors and is repeated three times. One actor has the cart and is shopping in the store, and the second actor enters the store and discovers the first actor. In each of the three separate takes, the entering actor will behave differently towards the shopping actor. Before entering, the actor will select someone from their personal life that they have (or have had) a *relationship* with and *transfer* their behavior from that *relationship* to their interaction with the shopping actor. The selected person should be different for each of the three entrances.

The entering actor must be specific about the *relationship* they are sourcing. General feelings, such as, "It's someone I like a lot," won't work. Actors need to select a specific person. It is *as if* the shopping actor is the person from their personal life that they have thought about.

For example, if I think about my *relationship* with Uta Hagen, who I admired and respected but also felt intimidated by, then I might play these *actions* to the shopping actor: *to idolize, to worship, to respect*, etc. Also, I might find it difficult to articulate my thoughts (*to struggle, to stumble* verbally and physically.) Actors should not reveal their sources. I am revealing my source only for the purpose of this example.

Furthermore, it is important that actors don't try to impose the physical image of their source onto the shopping actor. Actors are not trying to see that person. Instead, actors are looking to *transfer* their behavior—through verbal, non-verbal, psychological, and physical *action*—from their source to the shopping actor in order to discover the onstage *relationship*.

Following the first entrance and exchange, I stop the exercise and ask the shopping actor, "What is the nature of the *relationship* you just experienced?" Then, I ask the class what they saw. It is important not to let the class comments devolve into a discussion that seeks to make up a backstory about the *relationship*.

For example, if a student says, "They were lovers and there was a breakup," then I shift the discussion back to what we actually saw: "I saw a history to this *relationship* and how it is now uncomfortable." While it may be tempting to create a backstory, it is best to avoid a discussion about the story line, which is not important. The exercise is about exploring human behavior and the diverse *relationships* between people, not about the characters' backstories.

Next, I ask the entering actor, "How close are we in figuring out the *relationship* that you were working for?" Again, I don't want to know the actual source of an actor's *transfer* and warn actors not to reveal it.

Finally, the same process is repeated for the other two entrances. These encounters should be short. Then, after the three entrances, the roles are reversed: the shopping actor becomes the entering actor and the entering actor becomes the shopper.

The concept of *transference* also can be used for other aspects of our work, such as *place, circumstances*, needs, *obstacles*, etc. In order to make the work personal for our characters, we need to draw from our own lives and *transfer* those experiences to the play.

When working with *transfers*, the key words are "it is *as if*," e.g., it is *as if* my emotional *relationship* with my Aunt Gertrude is the same as Nonno's emotional *relationship* with his granddaughter, Hannah, in *The Night of the Iguana*. This technique is great for finding specific, personal *relationships* in our work. By bringing personal, life experience to their work, actors can make their characters' *relationships* personal and organic rather than intellectual.

◄ ALTERNATE SOURCES ►

THERE MAY BE TIMES when an actor can't find a source in a personal reference or *relationship* from their life experience. In that case, actors can take character traits from a variety of different people they know and combine them to create a single person.

Another technique involves using the imagination to construct a particular person or event. Actors can imagine the specific physical and psychological details of a human being and use that as a source.

For example, when I played the brilliant physicist Richard Feynman in *QED* by Peter Parnell, I (as Feynman) talked about my first wife, Arlene, who died of tuberculosis at the age of twenty-five. I created, through my visualization of her, every detail about her life: her height, weight, hairstyle, and eye color; the clothes she liked to wear; how we met and the places we lived; her health problems; and the things we did together.

In the play I discussed the details of her death—of her last breath. There was a sense of loss, but I (as Feynman) was devoid of an emotional response. I was protecting myself by absorbing the scientific details of her death:

> It was several months before I could react emotionally to her death. Not that I didn't feel it deeply. But it wasn't sinking in, until—isn't it interesting, how the mind works!—I was in Oak Ridge, and I was walking past a department store with dresses in the window, and I saw a pretty dress, and I thought, Arlene would like that. And it hit me ... It was too much for me.

As Feynman I was not prepared to see that dress and visualize, in my mind, Arlene wearing it. I was just walking down the street, looking in store windows. Catching a glimpse of the dress was unpredicted; it was spontaneous. Briefly, it seemed *as if* nothing tragic had happened—that Arlene was still alive. The moment was an emotional release, and the dress was the trigger. It was unprotected and unguarded, and it opened an emotional door that had been closed for several months.

As a scientist, Feynman analyzed all the physical facts of Arlene's illness, and he understood that she was dying. He was prepared for it. Feynman, however, was not prepared to see the dress.

The particular dress I used as my source contained a blue top and a white pleated skirt. Every time I played the scene, I visually connected to that dress and saw Arlene wearing it. This visualization and particularization process contained all of the details that were internally connected to Arlene as I verbally dealt with her memory.

I made this choice of particularization as a result of Parnell's writings, which detailed the *relationship* between Feynman and Arlene. Also, I read Feynman's love letter to Arlene, written two years after her death, which helped me further understand the depth of their *relationship*.

Then, while studying the play, I began to visualize Arlene, and she became very real for me. I soon realized that I couldn't come up with a better source for Arlene. Therefore, my research served as the springboard for my imagination.

Just as I did in this example, actors can create the specific details of what they need and then visualize those details, whether they relate to a person or an event. For me, these details did not stay on a piece of paper in my notebook; they became inner objects that I connected to every time I played the scene.

‹ EMOTIONAL TRIGGERS ›

AS HUMAN BEINGS, WE function well when we are in control of a situation. We feel secure, and it is easy to cope. But if something happens to which we are forced to cede control, then we find ourselves unable to function normally and desperately try to regain a sense of normalcy.

For example, many years ago I was involved in an automobile accident. When I exited the car and tried to walk, I felt some pain in left leg. Despite the wrecked car and my injured leg, the only thing I could think about was how I wanted to return to my apartment, remove the marinating chicken from the refrigerator, and prepare dinner. I wanted to engage in an activity that I could control—that would help me regain a sense of normalcy. Instead, I spent the next week in the hospital.

This fight for normalcy is apparent in the character Richard Feynman in *QED* as he tries to protect himself and stay in control following the death of his wife, Arlene. Scientifically, he has analyzed the physical facts of Arlene's death but has yet to deal with the emotional aspects of losing her. It isn't until he accidentally sees the dress—which he thinks would look good on her—in a store window that his suppressed emotions are released. The dress, therefore, served as an unprotected sensory trigger.

This discovery of unprotected sensory triggers is something with which we are all familiar. When telling a story about an emotional event to someone, we connect both verbally and sensorially to the event's surrounding details: the weather conditions, a piece of music that was playing, a stain on a tablecloth, an article of clothing, a particular smell, etc.

Then, before reaching the story's climax, we connect to one of the surrounding details and begin to uncontrollably laugh or cry, almost to the point where we are unable to finish the story. We have connected to an unprotected sensory trigger, which released the emotion.

That unintentional trigger can be a valuable tool for actors when used intentionally and woven into the given *circumstances* of a play. By using triggers that come directly from their life experiences, actors can connect to that sensory trigger as an inner object (thought) and thereby release the desired (and authentic) emotion.

It is important for actors not to think about the actual event, e.g., tears that result from the loss of a loved one or uncontrolled fits of laughter during a serious church sermon. Instead, actors should think about the surrounding sensory details of an event and discover the specific one that triggers the desired emotion.

For example, while working on this book with my friend Mary (yes, the same Mary from class), who was helping correct spelling and grammar errors that spell-check might have missed, we discovered one such instance. I wanted to use the phrase "touched the flag." Instead, I mistyped "torched the flag," which completely changed the meaning of the sentence and went undetected by spell-check. As we laughed at that typing error, I was reminded of something that happened when I was studying with Uta Hagen at HB Studio.

As a scholarship student, I was required to monitor her beginning class by taking attendance and making a list of the scenes, exercises, and monologues that the students were presenting in class that day. One day, after finishing the list, I placed it on Ms. Hagen's desk. She then entered the classroom, picked up the list, and read my spelling mistakes to the class. Everyone laughed.

While retelling this forgotten story to Mary, I felt my face flush with embarrassment. I had connected to the little table in the back of the classroom where I sat—and to Ms. Hagen holding my list at a distance from her eyes. Some fifty years later, those triggers made me blush.

I could have used those triggers when I played the old man in Craig Lucas' fairy tale play *Prelude to a Kiss*. As my character kissed the bride, Rita, at her wedding, Rita's soul and the old man's magically exchanged bodies. I believed that I was the young bride, and she believed that she was the old man. While trying to solve this mystery, the groom, Peter, kissed me, attempting to ascertain if I truly was his bride.

At that moment, if I had connected to those triggers from long ago (my little table and Ms. Hagen picking up my list)—and wove them into my inner objects in connection with the given *circumstances* of the play—then I would have blushed. Thus, triggers are valuable tools for actors. (See "The Psychological Senses" in Uta Hagen's *A Challenge for the Actor* for more information about *transfers* and triggers.)

‹ EVALUATION 15: CHANGES OF SELF EXERCISE (PART TWO) ›

JAN PRESENTS PART Two of Uta Hagen's Changes of Self Exercise, which involves getting dressed for an event. She sets up a living room and enters from outside carrying a garment bag. It appears *as if* she is tired and in a bad mood. After dropping the garment bag on the couch, Jan sits down next to it, leans back, and closes her eyes. Moments later, she sits up, grabs a magazine from the coffee table, and thumbs through it. No longer interested in the magazine, Jan throws it off the table and onto the floor. She doesn't seem to care and leaves it there.

Next, the garment bag catches Jan's attention, and she unzips it, revealing the black Persian lamb fur coat contained inside. She feels the texture of the coat, which is pleasant for her, and slowly puts on the coat. Immediately, Jan starts to transform. Her fatigue fades, as does her bad mood. By the time she finishes putting on the coat, Jan is a different person. It's clear that she feels good and has a new lease on life. Now, she is ready and confident as she makes her exit to the party, which she originally did not want to attend.

ME: Jan, how did you feel?

JAN: Good. I didn't think I could do this without looking in a mirror. I see what you mean about the feeling. It is what the coat did to me, not how I looked in it.

ME: Right. The coat took you to another part of you. You showed that you could play that self-assured, confident character, and it was coming from your behavior in that coat. You were not illustrating the character. It was coming from you and your fur coat. Good work, Jan.

Each of us has experienced the act of putting on a particular article of clothing and feeling differently. For me, it may be my t-shirt that has shrunk so much that it will barely tuck into my pants. Every time I bend over, it rides up and comes out of my pants. It makes me feel irritable and stupid and affects how I move and relate.

Or perhaps it's my large, white cotton summer shirt, imported from Turkey, that I bought in Provincetown twenty years ago. It easily slips on over my head and just hangs. The cotton is thick and nubby, and its texture is soft and rough. While wearing it, I feel daring, self-assured, sexy, and ready for a good time. Each of these garments bring out a different part of *me*.

NOTE TO ACTORS: When working on this exercise, do not use a mirror. This exercise is not about how you *look*; it is about how you *feel*. If you look in a mirror, then you run the risk of destroying the feeling.

◀ EVALUATION 16: *COLLECTED STORIES* (SCENE) ▶

JEANNIE AND STEPHANIE PRESENT the first scene from *Collected Stories* by Donald Margulies, on which they have worked previously. (In Class Three Jeannie presented a monologue from the play, playing the same character: Ruth.)

For the rework, I had asked Jeannie (as Ruth) to pull back on her *relationship* with Lisa. It seemed that she was purposely playing the upper hand in order to intimidate Lisa, who seemed to take the encounter a little too casually. I also asked both Jeannie and Stephanie to consider what was at stake for each of their characters.

The rework was much improved. The *relationship* between teacher (Ruth) and student (Lisa) was solid. We saw Lisa process her first encounter with Ruth, which was discovered internally with few words. At first, Lisa seemed insecure but gradually gained confidence when her mentor, Ruth, seemed to express approval and a positive response to Lisa's work. For both actors, the *action* work was clean and specific. The scene was well rehearsed and received several laughs.

ME: How did you feel?

JEANNIE: Good.

STEPHANIE: Yes, it was fun. I didn't expect those laughs.

ME: Why did we laugh? This is not Neil Simon, with a set up and joke.

STEPHANIE: We identified.

ME: Yes. We, somehow, have been there. We know what Lisa is going through, and we laugh. This is the basis for all humor. There is something universal and human happening, and we understand it. We are laughing at ourselves.

Jeannie, one thing you need to do is relax your verbal *actions*. Give more attention to Lisa. See and listen to her in detail. Allow her to be different every time. This will keep you alive in your performance, and your perceptions of her will be a little different each performance. It will be fun for you as an actor.

When Paul Muni was in *Inherit the Wind*, another player told him that there was a problem with her costume, and she, as a result, would be wearing a different blouse for the performance that night. He responded, "I wish you hadn't told me. I would have liked to discover that in the scene."

Jeannie, for you, right now everything is set—is predetermined—and framed in your mind. It will always be the same. You need to let it change, depending on what you are picking up from Stephanie, which will be different every performance. You need to work on this.

Once you find a good verbal *action*, you tend to freeze it. Stay loose with it. You won't lose the *action*. Sometimes it will be stronger. And there will be times where it won't be as strong, depending on how you perceive the moment. Keep it in the present tense, and you will make new discoveries. Good theatre is alive. The moment theatre becomes frozen, it is dead. If there is no difference as to how an actor plays an *action*, from the stage or at home in the shower, then that *action* is dead.

Another thing: those derogatory remarks you directed to Lisa—about paying attention to the seating charts—try directing them to yourself.

Immediately, Jeannie ran over that section again and saw exactly what I was talking about. It changed her *actions*, and as a result, we saw a different part of Ruth.

◄ EVALUATION 17: FINDING OCCUPATION WHILE WAITING ►

MARILYN IS A PROFESSIONAL actor who does a lot of stage work. When she isn't working, she takes classes and has been working her way through the Hagen exercises. Here, she presents the seventh exercise: Finding Occupation while Waiting.

In her first presentation, Marilyn, wearing an outdoor jacket and carrying a few things (I can't tell what they are by the way she is holding them), enters an empty space. She stands there for a minute (or so), looking at something ahead of her. Then, she mimes placing the objects onto something I can't see, and says, "Scene."

ME: How did you feel?

MARILYN: I just put this together this morning. I know—it needs work. I will put more time in it for next week.

ME: Marilyn, where are you? Are you outdoors?

MARILYN: No. I was in a super market. I wanted to use the shopping cart, but I couldn't find it.

ME: It's back there in the prop area. But for this exercise, I'm glad that you didn't find it. The shopping cart is such a strong object to work with. It would have eliminated the acting problem in the exercise. That object, the shopping cart, would have given you involvement and occupation. This exercise is not about having things around you to work with. While you are waiting, you need to find what you are doing physically and what you are dealing with internally. When you explore these areas, you will be occupied.

In this exercise, you shouldn't have furniture to go to … or lots of objects to work with. It's all about what do we do physically when we are waiting for someone on a street corner—and what our thought process is, which can go anywhere depending on what is going on in our lives at this moment in time while we are waiting.

When Marilyn presents the exercise to the class the following week, her situation is completely different. This time, she sets a single chair center stage and enters wearing the same jacket. It appears *as if* she is looking for something. She seems impatient. Eventually, Marilyn sits in the chair, and we see a variety of different expressions on her face. After a few moments, she stands and says, "Scene."

ME: How did you feel?

MARILYN: Better, but it still wasn't right.

ME: Marilyn, you don't trust yourself.

MARILYN: You are right.

ME: You are doing too much and end up overcompensating. You are trying to make it interesting for the audience. Don't do that. Trust that if you simply look to see where the bus is coming from, it will be enough. If you simply think about what is going on in your life while you are waiting, then you will feel involved and occupied as human—and that will be communicated to the audience. In fact, it will be compelling to watch.

MARILYN: I will rework it for next week.

In her final rework, Marilyn sets up the same location as the previous week. She enters, looks stage left, and then looks at the ground. Obviously impatient, she shifts her weight from foot to foot and looks stage left again before eventually sitting in the chair. Once seated, she looks left again and then ahead. A small smile appears on her face as she removes a change purse from her pocket and counts the change. She then puts the change back in her pocket and the change purse in a separate pocket. After a long pause, we can tell that something is going on inside her head, and we wonder what she is thinking. Eventually, she stands, takes the change from her pocket, and says, "Scene"

ME: Marilyn, how did you feel?

MARILYN: Good.

ME: It was wonderful, Marilyn. You must have been aware of how we were responding to your work. It was so quiet in the studio—you could have heard a pin drop. We were riveted to you. This is a lesson for all of us: simple involvement and occupation is spellbinding. Thank you, Marilyn.

The problems Marilyn dealt with in this exercise come up in a lot of productions. Actors are asked to stand on an empty stage for a lengthy period of time, typically waiting for another character to arrive or an event to happen.

Often, actors feel self-conscious and too aware of the audience. They try to fix their bodies by finding interesting ways of standing, all while wondering what the audience might be thinking.

Uta Hagen solves this problem by helping actors find physical and inner occupation while waiting, which is what we do in real life. Think about all the things we do physically, and the things we think about, while we are waiting for someone or something.

In Ms. Hagen's directions for this exercise, actors are required to stand. Actors and humans are vulnerable when standing. However, I didn't mention this to Marilyn since she was able to solve the acting problem while seated and learn Ms. Hagen's lesson, which will change her work dramatically.

CHAPTER 9

~

WORKING WITH STUDENTS WITH DISABLITIES

IT IS ESTIMATED THAT roughly fifty million Americans (or one in five) live with a disability. I suffer from chronic obstructive pulmonary disease (COPD), which limits my physical activity. I am on oxygen therapy as needed. My disability has made it difficult for me to act. However, I am interested in playing the lead character, an old man confined to a wheelchair who is dealing with his own mortality, in *Wakey Wakey* by Will Eno.

Fortunately, my disability doesn't affect my teaching since I am not the type of teacher that actively demonstrates. Nor does it diminish my creative drive, which is an important thing to remember when working with students with disabilities.

There is no correct or exact way to describe what works best when teaching students with disabilities: each student has their own set of unique circumstances. As a result, I deal with each student on a case-by-case basis and attempt to provide as many accommodations as possible for students with disabilities.

If an individual's disability requires them to move or speak at a slower rate, I try to be patient and considerate. When it appears necessary, I offer physical assistance to students with disabilities. But if they prefer to be independent and decline the offer, then it is important to be respectful of that choice.

Disability advocates emphasize the necessity of using respectful terminology. In the studio I cannot stress enough times the importance of practicing and promoting disability etiquette, which includes referring to a student as a "person with a disability," rather than a "disabled person."

This language also should be applied to specific disabilities. For instance, saying "person who is blind" is more respectful than saying "blind person." By putting the "person" first, it identifies the individual as a fellow human being, rather than someone defined solely by a disability.

◀ WORKING WITH JENNIFER ▶

JENNIFER, WHO HAS STUDIED with me off and on for many years, suffers from an extremely rare disorder of the retina, a gradually progressive condition that makes her eyes sensitive to light. As a result, she is unable to read regular sized print without magnification. If a piece is short, such as an exercise or a monologue, it can be easily typed-up and converted to a digital format where she can use the accessibility features of an iPad to make it easier to read. I worked with Jennifer on a Rumi poem, "The Sheikh Who Lost Two Sons," which she wanted to read at a memorial for a deceased friend. She did a beautiful reading of this insightful work.

Play scripts, however, present a problem for Jennifer since the small font size is difficult—if not impossible—to read. I suggested that Jennifer contact Dramatists Play Service or Samuel French to inquire about the availability of play scripts for visually impaired actors. She was pleasantly surprised to learn that both companies offer plays in a digital format. She is now able to work on scenes with other actors.

Jennifer's vision impairment also makes it difficult for her to make eye contact with other actors during large, group exercises. She requests that other actors gesture to her with a slight nod of the head in addition to looking at her. During one such exercise, as its pace increased, Jennifer withdrew, believing that she would slow things down. Protests from the class followed. The other actors insisted that she stay in the group. "Richard Alan sets the tone for what I would describe as a sacred space for creativity," Jennifer observed. "He brings forth the same behavior in the actors in class."

‹ WORKING WITH ERIN ›

OTHER STUDENTS WITH DISABILITIES require different approaches. Take Erin, an aspiring actor with Asperger syndrome, a neurobiological disorder on the higher functioning end of the autism spectrum. People with Asperger syndrome can present a variety of symptoms and behaviors, but typically, they experience problems with social and communications skills.

When Erin first came to class, she proclaimed, "I want to act." She previously had been working with Cynthia Hyer (a professional Kansas City actor) on a monologue from a Harry Potter book. Cynthia was helping Erin with her voice and diction. For the next class, Erin read the passage that she had been working on with Cynthia. Her voice and diction were good.

Then, in an attempt to bring the piece to life by using her imagination, I had her read the passage to Cooper and encouraged her to make eye contact with him. She seemed to enjoy the experience. We repeated this exercise for the next class.

However, retrospectively, I think a different approach might have worked better. Instead of having Erin read the monologue directly to Cooper, I should have asked her to think of someone to whom she would like to tell, not read, the story. Then, with a specific person—who she could *transfer* onto Cooper—in mind, her *objective* would have been clearer: *to entertain* that person with this great Harry Potter story. I believe the results would have been better. Working with students with a disability is a learning process for both teacher and student.

Next, I assigned Erin a scene from *The Glass Menagerie* by Tennessee Williams, with her playing Laura. She liked the scene where Laura tells her mother how in high school Jim called her "Blue Roses." Nancy, a superb professional actor, offered to play Amanda, Laura's mother.

Erin and Nancy worked on the scene for three weeks. Nancy brought in an old leg brace, and Erin used it to help define the specific location of Laura's limp. Additionally, Erin worked on listening and personally digesting what her acting partner was saying to her. Erin also found a source for Jim, the high school boy on whom she had a crush. The scene work was a success, and Erin's confidence grew.

Interestingly, Erin wasn't the first actress with a disability to play Laura. In a 2017 production directed by Sam Gold, Laura was played by Madison Ferris, who has muscular dystrophy. Not only was Ferris making her Broadway debut opposite Oscar-winner Sally Field as Amanda, she became the first actress in a wheelchair to land a leading role. "I feel like it should have happened sooner," she told People Magazine. "In the long run, I just feel like an actor trying to do the part as best I can."

◄ EVALUATION 18: *THE CURIOUS INCIDENT ...* (SCENE) ►

ERIN WAS ASSIGNED A scene from *The Curious Incident of the Dog in the Night-Time* by Simon Stephens, adapted from the novel by Mark Haddon. In the play, Christopher, a teen boy with autism and a savant in math, is trying to solve the mystery of why a dog was stabbed to death with a pitch fork in the nighttime. In this scene I am not asking Erin to play a boy. Instead, we will call her character Chris, and she will play Chris as herself. Jon will work with Erin and play the minister, who is trying to answer Chris' questions about the location of heaven. Following the first read, I discussed it with Erin.

ME: Erin, how did you feel?

ERIN: Pretty good.

ME: Erin you are going to have to research black holes. I don't know what they are, so you'll have to explain them to me.

ERIN: I know what they are. Black holes are created when a star implodes. After it's been dying for a while, it becomes like a supernova. And sometimes it just becomes a black hole and everything gets sucked into it, including light.

ME: It's like a vacuum cleaner.

ERIN: Yeah, a bit. And that's all I know so far.

ME: Excellent. Where does this scene take place?

ERIN: At school.

ME: Where? What room in school?

ERIN: It doesn't say.

ME: Use your imagination. It is it a classroom? Or maybe the minister's office?

ERIN: His office.

ME: Okay, good. Let's set up his office and read it again.

They set up an office with desk, chairs, couch, books, computer, telephone, etc.

ME: Now, let's have you make an entrance and knock on the door. Your *objective* is *to prove* to him that there is no heaven.

Erin worked with Jon on the scene for several weeks and had a good time. She was animated and enjoyed possessing the knowledge of how the universe operates; she also enjoyed making the minister uncomfortable. This play was an excellent choice for Erin: she could identify with and personally relate to the character of Chris.

In the same class Erin worked with a new student, Troy, on Exercise Ten: Side-Coached Actions. Erin was playing the employment office worker, and Troy was playing the applicant. When provided the verb *to teach*, Troy tried *to teach* Erin how to reorganize her desk in order to make her workflow more efficient. Then, Erin was provided the verb *to avoid*. She immediately looked at the papers on her desk, rolled her eyes, and sarcastically proclaimed, "Whatever." The class burst into laughter and applause.

CHAPTER 10

~

ADDITIONAL
EXERCISES

THESE ADDITIONAL EXERCISES EXPOSE actors to specific acting problems and can be used at the discretion of teachers. Many of my students have found these exercises valuable.

◄ EXERCISE 15: ACTION DISCOVERY ►

THIS EXERCISE USES SHAKESPEARE's lines from Hamlet's soliloquy ("To be or not to be") and requires that actors be proficient in verbal and psychological *action* work. I developed this exercise—at the request of actors—to address an additional acting problem not dealt with in Exercise Seven, the original "To be or not to be" exercise: what to do with the sensation experienced when an actor receives a verb from another actor.

In Exercise Seven, since all actors are playing the same verb for every word of "To be or not to be," actors—in order to send that same verb to the next actor—must discard their emotional responses after receiving the verb. This exercise seeks to remedy that problem.

To begin, actors form a circle, either sitting or standing, in the workspace. Next, I privately assign a verb to a student. For example, I might give Elizabeth the verb *to demand*. Using *transference*, she takes the time to decide exactly who she is demanding and what she is demanding them to do. Once Elizabeth has established her *transfer*, she selects an actor (in this case Dan), focuses her attention on him, and says, "To," sending him the verb (*action*) *to demand* behind it.

Dan receives the verb—and depending upon the sensation he experiences—sends (possibly) a different verb to another actor (or maybe even the same actor) with the second word of the line, "Be." His *action* might be *to challenge, to rebuff, to deny, to accuse, to attack, to defend*, etc. His verb is played based on his emotional and/or intellectual response to what he received from Elizabeth.

After finishing the last word in the line ("question"), we discuss how actors came up with the verb they selected to play, much like we did with clerk character in Exercise Eight: The Shoe Store. This exercise is about sending and receiving *actions*, with the receiving actors openly receiving what is being played to them and then, depending on what sensation they experience, subsequently sending out the next verb. It is important that actors not pre-determine the verb that they are going to send. Actors need to leave themselves open to experience a truthful sensation that results from what they receive from their partner and subsequently discover when sending the next verb to another actor. *Acting is doing.*

When rehearsing scenes, actors should use a similar technique when approaching how they discover and play verbs. Actors should not preset verbs prior to rehearsal. Instead, they must open themselves to receive their next moment of life from their acting partner, thereby organically discovering the next verb that they will play. After rehearsal, actors should pencil in the verbs that worked, which will help them in finalizing the *action* score for the scene.

◄ EXERCISE 16: THE KNOWN AND THE UNKNOWN (PART II) ►

THIS EXERCISE REQUIRES TWO characters: Character A and Character B. A living room is set up with an outside door, couch, chairs, and coffee table with books, magazines, and other objects. I ask the students to write down the following physical *actions* and dialogue:

Character A is at home reading. Character B knocks on the door. Character A stands up and opens the door.

CHARACTER B

Hi or hello. (Actor's choice.)

CHARACTER A

Hi or hello. (Actor's choice.)

CHARACTER B

Are you going to ask me in?

CHARACTER A

Oh. Sure. Come in. (Note the punctuation.)

(*Character B enters.*)

CHARACTER B

How are you?

CHARACTER A

I'm fine.

CHARACTER B

You look fine.

CHARACTER A

Would you like to sit down?

CHARACTER B

Sure.

I select Taylor to play Character B and Andrea to play Character A and ask the two actors to run the dialogue a few times, until they are familiar with it. In this exercise the characters have opposing *objectives* and should explore verbal, non-verbal, physical, and psychological *action*.

Next, I have a private conversation with Taylor, who is playing character B. He needs to define the *relationship* between the two characters, his *objective* (the reason for knocking on the door), and what verb he is going to play in relationship to his *objective*.

It is very important for Taylor to commit to the *circumstances*, *relationship*, *objectives*, and *actions* of the exercise. My off-stage conversation with Taylor:

ME: What's the *relationship* between you and Andrea?

TAYLOR: She is my ex-girlfriend.

ME: Why are you coming to see her?

TAYLOR: I want to get back together.

ME: Why did you break-up?

TAYLOR: She caught me with her best friend.

ME: What's your verb?

TAYLOR: *To plead.*

Before we begin, I remind Andrea, who is playing Character A, that her *objective* will be in opposition to Taylor's *objective*. In a similar real-life situation, actors would explore more than one verb, but for the purpose of this exercise, we are dealing with only one. And similar to Exercise Eight: The Shoe Store, Character B has predetermined their verb while Character A discovers their *objective* and verbs spontaneously.

In this exercise actors deal with several problems. First, actors must deliver the dialogue, which has nothing to do with what is happening in the scene; the scene is all about subtext. Next, Character B is challenged by having to play the same verb throughout the scene, which requires discipline. Finally, many actors play the situation rather than the actual verb they have chosen. When actors play the situation, they are not playing *actions*; they are playing moods and emotional generalities. When actors play their verb, *actions* become specific and a possible emotional release will follow. Actors should fight to control the emotional release and put it into *action*.

During the exercise, actors should take as much time with the dialogue as needed. Since this exercise is not about the words, a lot can happen in between the lines. Sometimes, I will have the actors repeat the exercise until they effectively land their verb.

Even though no additional dialogue exists after the last line ("Sure"), the scene is not over until I stop it. During this time, actors should explore non-verbal *actions*. However, if they start to mime or make odd faces, then the scene should be stopped.

This exercise is not about story or plot. I am looking for what is happening humanly between these two characters, including the importance and exploration of non-verbal *action*.

I also look for what the actors are doing in relationship to each other. Even something as simple as the knock on the door can be a verb. Following the exercise, I ask Andrea what is going on in the scene.

ANDREA: He wants something from me.

ME: What do you think is the nature of the *relationship*?

ANDREA: We are close ... or were once close.

ME: What did he do to communicate that?

ANDREA: The way he knocked on the door. It was very soft, iffy. I opened the door. His look, especially his eyes, communicated a need. He wanted something. His embrace was tentative.

ME: What was your *objective*?

ANDREA: To withhold whatever he wants.

ME: What did you do?

ANDREA: I ended the embrace and put distance between us.

ME: What verb was he playing?

ANDREA: *To beg, to apologize, to grovel, to plead.*

ME: It is not important that you come up with the exact verb. Any verb in the ballpark will do.

After our discussion, Taylor explains to the class the details of the plot. Then, we reverse the situation—Andrea becomes Character B and Taylor Character A—and repeat the exercise. Each actor in class will have the opportunity to work on both characters.

◄ EXERCISE 17: CHANGING PREVIOUS CIRCUMSTANCES ►

THIS EXERCISE DEMONSTRATES THE importance of working on the immediate previous *circumstances* prior to making an entrance. It relates to the Destination Exercise and is worked on the same way, except the actor will make two separate entrances. In each entrance the previous *circumstances* should be different.

For example, in my first entrance I come into the kitchen from the outdoors after working in the yard on a hot summer day. It is 3:30 p.m. on Wednesday, July 23rd, and I am sweating. I grab a towel, wet it with cold water, and wrap it around my neck. Next, I open the fridge, remove a bottle of ice water, and pour it into a glass. Finally, I sit down and take a drink.

Entrance two begins off stage, where I put on a bathrobe and slippers before entering the kitchen from the bathroom. It is 5:30 a.m. on Thursday, December 13th, and I am cold. Barely awake, I turn on the kitchen light, wrap the bathrobe around me to keep warm, and turn on the coffee pot. While waiting for the coffee, I heat a couple of cups of water for a few seconds in the microwave to warm them, try to wipe the sleep from my eyes, and remove the cups from the microwave. I place one of the cups on the counter, sit down, and sip hot water from the other cup while waiting for the coffee to finish brewing.

In both of these examples, the on stage *action* is approximately the same. However, the execution of the *action* is different as a result of the different physical conditions that arose from the immediate previous *circumstances*. After entering the kitchen simply to get a drink, my behavior changes based upon the two different sets of previous *circumstances*.

◄ EXERCISE 18: OBJECT TRANSFORMATION ►

IN THIS EXERCISE ACTORS sit in a circle on the floor. I select an actor, Terry, to begin. I tell Terry that there is an imaginary mound of clay on the floor in front of him and ask him to put his hands into this substance. He starts working with the clay and shaping it, until it becomes an object. It might become a hat, a bowl, a mug, etc. It is important for Terry not to think about what he is doing and let his hands organically discover the object while playing with the clay. It's much like doodling with a pencil and paper.

Once Terry's object is complete, he passes it to the actor on his right, Susie, and says, "Susie, I am giving you a hat." Susie then physically explores Terry's hat before eventually transforming it to a new object. She should not destroy the hat but rather bend the brim and start to reshape the rest of the hat, thus discovering a new object—in this case a rocket (but it could be anything). When her rocket is fully formed, Susie passes it to the actor on her right, Ellen, and says, "Ellen, I am giving you a rocket." Ellen repeats the process of exploring the rocket and transforming it into a new object.

As the imaginary object moves around the circle, actors—when they receive the object—should not destroy it and start over from scratch. Instead, they should experience the joy of discovery by allowing the object to transform into something new. It is important for actors not to predetermine the object they will create

Just as in Exercise Two: The Mirror, actors are working together, much like they would during a scene when an actor sends an *action* to their partner, who receives that *action* and then sends it back in a new form.

The exercise ends when the object completes its way around the circle and returns to the first actor, Terry, who will make one final transformation. Finally, I ask each actor to talk about the process of discovering, evolving, and transforming the object.

◄ EXERCISE 19: SOUND AND MOTION ►

THIS EXERCISE ORIGINATED WITH The Open Theatre, an experimental theatre founded by Nola Chilton and Joe Chaiken that operated from 1963-1973.

To begin, actors form a standing circle. I select an actor—in this example, John—to enter the center of the circle, which is now his workspace. John invents and explores both an abstract sound and a physical motion. He can start with either the sound or the motion— or delve into both simultaneously.

If he starts exploring the motion first, then the sound should evolve naturally—or vice versa. When satisfied with his choices, John moves to another actor in the circle: Kathy, in this example. He stands in front of her, repeating both the sound and motion (at the same time) until she joins him, mirroring his sound and motion. Once she is secure with it, Kathy changes places with John, moves to the center of the circle, and gradually transforms his sound and motion into a new one of her own. As Kathy's new sound and motion takes over, John fades out with his. Kathy then finds another actor and repeats the process.

When the last actor, Tangela, is reached, she discovers a new sound and motion and then takes it to the first actor, John. Tangela and John then mirror each other and take that sound and motion to different actors around the circle, sharing it until the entire class is doing Tangela's sound and motion, which should incorporate an element of each previous actor's sound and motion. As each actor becomes involved in this final part, the excitement and energy will build until it reaches a climax.

This exercise takes actors back to childhood, when we invented sounds and movements simply because we could. Not only is this exercise fun, it also helps actors shed their preconceived self-images.

Note the similarity this exercise has with Exercise 2: The Mirror and Exercise 18: Object Transformation. It would be ideal for actors to work on and present these exercises consecutively. The three exercises emphasize the importance of working together and the exchange of creative energy from one actor to another—and eventually to the ensemble—through transformations.

As actors, we transform ourselves into the characters we play; we transform our environments, clothes, *relationships*, *objectives*, and *actions* into personal doings, which is crucial to our work on stage.

◄ EXERCISE 20: EMOTIONAL TRIGGERS ►

THIS EXERCISE DEMONSTRATES AN actor's use of a personal life experience, which can be *transferred* to their *relationships* with the other characters, objects, events, and environments in a play. Students might consider exploring this exercise after working on Exercise 14: Use of Self-Transference (see Class Six). It should be rehearsed at home and brought into class for evaluation.

First, an actor selects one primary object to connect with physically, psychologically, and emotionally and decides their *relationship* to the object based on a personal life experience. It must be a real object, such as a book, a letter, a drinking glass, an article of clothing, etc. In addition to the primary object, other secondary objects should be placed throughout (or brought into) the room for the actor to deal with prior to discovering the primary object.

Next, an actor makes an entrance into a room of their choice (much like the Destination Exercise), where they will discover and relate to the primary object, which does not have to be used for its primary purpose: the actor is simply discovering the object. The reason for the entrance should be a routine *objective*: to pay bills, to clean the room, to rearrange the furniture, etc.

For example, suppose I have chosen a blue scarf as my primary object, my office work area as the entrance destination, and opening the mail as my *objective*. Then, I enter my office work area with the just delivered mail. But before I can complete my *objective* (opening the mail), I notice the blue scarf—my primary object—draped over the back of a chair. I place the mail on the desk and approach the scarf. Perhaps its color reminds me of a personal life experience, which I can draw upon as the source for my *relationship* to the primary object: the blue scarf.

When recalling this personal life experience, I pay close attention to the secondary elements of the experience (the surrounding sensory details): a visual recollection of something I saw, the weather conditions, a piece of music that was playing, a particular smell, etc. These elements are unprotected and will open the door to the emotion experienced at the time of the event. (See Class Six: Emotional Triggers). For me personally, visual details work best.

The Radio, Laughter, and an Emotional Trigger

WHEN MY BROTHER WAS five years old (I was seven), he nearly drowned. It was a rainy Sunday, until around seven in the evening, when the sky began to clear. We had gone with our parents to visit their friends at a house on a nearby fish hatchery. They said that we could play outside but instructed us not to go down to the fish pools. I, of course, had a better idea.

"Let's sneak down to the fish pools," I said to my brother, who was wearing a blue sweater that my mother had knitted for him. "They will never know."

There were several pools of fish, and my brother was fascinated by a particular fish. To get a closer look, he stepped down the steep bank leading to that pool. The wet grass and mud caused him to slip and fall head first into the pool. He didn't know how to swim.

I ran back to the house as fast as I could and entered the living room, where my mother and her friend were knitting and listening to the radio. "Mom! Mom! Bobby fell in a fish pool and is learning how to swim," I informed her.

She screamed in panic and called to my father, who was in another part of the house talking business with the man who managed the hatchery. The two men immediately ran down to the pools. At first, they couldn't find my brother. Then, my father's friend spotted a blue sweater at the bottom of one of the pools. He dove in, pulled out my brother, and started CPR. Soon, the fire department arrived and took over. My brother was fine, but he had to spend the night in the hospital.

While recalling the surrounding details related to the sensory elements of this event, I discovered an emotional trigger: a console radio—with red and green lights—that was in the living room of the fish hatchery house. When I entered the living room to alert my mom about my drowning brother, the radio was broadcasting a program with Edgar Bergen and Charlie McCarthy, and I remember hearing people laughing. The laughter was such a dramatic contrast to what I was feeling at the time: fear, panic, and guilt.

Now that I have an emotional trigger (the radio and people laughing), in the exercise I will physically connect to the blue scarf and discover *actions* that explore my emotional and psychological *relationship* to it. In this example I clutch the scarf and hold on to it for dear life (the *action*), *as if* I am holding on to my brother.

It is important that I not predetermine my emotional response to the scarf but rather let it happen organically based upon my sensory connection to it as a result of my trigger.

Finally, once I have connected to the scarf, my closing *action* is to exit the room with the scarf. My exit should be to a specific destination, must have purpose, and should reflect my mental and emotional state after discovering the scarf. In this example I exit the room, return the scarf to the bedroom, and place it in the closet.

How to Use Triggers

Just as I did in the exercise, actors can imaginatively weave personal life experiences into a play. By contacting inner trigger objects and working with personal sources, actors can incorporate real and believable emotions into the given *circumstances* and events of a play.

For example, I can use that console radio with red and green lights and the sounds of people laughing as an inner object in any play that calls for my character to experience a major episode of fear, panic, and guilt. Once I have done all the personal work on my character—*relationships, objectives, circumstances,* and *actions*—then, in the scene that requires those specific emotions, I can weave the radio trigger into the *circumstances* of the play as an inner object, and it will produce the required emotions. I won't need to think consciously about my brother: the emotion will come from my subconscious.

NOTE TO ACTORS: It is not enough to discover a trigger that leads to an emotional release. You must be able to put that emotion into *action* (in the exercise example, clutching the scarf) by fighting for normalcy, which was why I exclaimed to my mother, "Mom! Mom! Bobby fell in a fish pool and is learning how to swim." At seven years old, in my struggle to maintain normalcy, I was unable to tell my mom that Bobby was in danger of drowning. All I could say was that he was "learning how to swim."

You should never drop out of the play and dwell on your personal, real life experience. The triggers need to be part of the play and should come from life experiences that you can control emotionally.

If you are intuitively, psychologically, and emotionally connected to the play on which you are working, then you may not need to use this technique. However, if a connection dries up for you during the course of the run of a play (or if you are having a problem with releasing emotion), then you may want to explore this technique.

This exercise can be repeated many times to discover multiple triggers.

NOTE TO TEACHERS: Don't ask your students what they are using as personal sources or triggers. I simply revealed mine in order to make this example realistic. When an actor publicly reveals a source, it will no longer work for them.

EPILOGUE

~

THE
PERFORMANCE

PRIOR TO THE OPENING of a play, rehearsals during tech week provide important time for actors to refine their craft. While the crew solves various problems that arise with lights, sound, sets, costumes, props etc., actors can work on a section over and over again until any problems or acting bugs are resolved. This extra time also presents actors an opportunity to make new discoveries in their work.

◄ SHOW DAY ►

EVERY ACTOR HAS THEIR own routine on performance day. I wake up in the morning knowing that the highlight of my day will start at seven-thirty that evening. During the day, I try to pace my energy. From time to time, my mind will step into the world of the play and go to my character. To make sure my lines are firmly planted in my brain, I spend, usually in the morning, anywhere from forty-five minutes to an hour on a speed run-through. I don't want to have that horrible experience of losing my words in front of an audience.

The equity call (for actors to arrive at the theatre and sign-in) is one half hour before the performance. I, however, try to arrive an hour to an hour and a half before the performance in order to organize the dressing room (or my space in a dressing area) and make sure my costumes are hanging in the proper order for my changes.

Next, I check the prop table for my props. Are they all there? If I can't find a prop, I make a note (or advise the stage manager) and then search the theatre if necessary. If I need a prop for my first entrance, I will take it with me back to the dressing room.

Then, I start the physical transformation into my character by putting on my character's trousers and shoes. If it is all right with the stage manager, I walk onto the set and start to transform it to my personal environment for the play by placing my fourth side points of focus, warming up my voice and body, and checking my vocal projection.

Finally, I return to the dressing room and finish putting on my costume, transforming it into the clothes I, as the character, am wearing. I have assigned a history and personal *relationship* to the clothes. I apply whatever make-up is needed. At my age, I need very little.

Throughout this pre-show process, I continue to step into the world of the play and leave behind my real life world in Kansas City. My goal, as I enter into the world of, for example, Sorin in *The Seagull*, is to find myself on my country estate in 1895 Russia.

While it would be wonderful if there were some peace and quiet backstage, there is usually a lot of chatter, gossip, joking around, etc. I try to ignore as much of that as possible, which is another reason why I arrive so early: to begin my transformation into character with as few distractions as possible.

‹ DURING THE SHOW ›

IF I AM ON stage when the performance starts, I make sure that I position myself with as little distance as possible to travel to my place on stage. Since it is dark, I use the glow tape to guide me to my place. Internally, I am connecting to my character's inner objects, which have been established in rehearsal. For each performance, I connect to them differently.

If I am making an entrance, I will use what I have learned from the Destination Exercise to establish where I am coming from, what I have been doing there, and why I am coming into this environment.

My goal is to play each scene in the present tense. It is *as if* the events of the play have never happened. By working in this manner, my inner objects vary, resulting in a slightly different performance each time. The physical movements and outer shape of my performance will be the same. Since I am a little different each day of my life, I bring that difference to the theatre and my performance. Internally, I improvise on those inner thoughts.

During the run of a show, it is important for actors not to use the same inner thoughts each night, *as if* they are repeating them by rote and recalling their inner thoughts without thinking about what is behind them. If actors work this way, their performances will get stuck in a rut. By varying inner objects (thoughts) for each performance, actors can bring new life to their characters, and their performances will grow more meaningful.

For example, Ms. Hagen once told a story about seeing Laurette Taylor play Amanda in *The Glass Menagerie*. She saw the play three or four times, and it was never exactly the same. Each performance was spellbinding.

One night, she took a friend, who had not seen the production, with her. Before a particular scene, Ms. Hagen said to her friend, "Wait till you see what Laurette does here." Whatever was supposed to happen didn't happen at that moment. It, instead, happened in the next beat. Laurette Taylor didn't demand that the emotion happen exactly the same way every performance. She allowed it to happen organically, when it was there. Emotion cannot be choreographed, and actors cannot command the same degree of emotion during every performance: sometimes it will be fuller than others. Since the performance is live, actors can only give what they are actually experiencing. Emotions should not be forced.

Any emotions actors experience must move the action of the play forward, otherwise it is just emotion for the sake of emotion. If emotion isn't channeled into a verb, then it is pointless. When emotion is done properly, some actors will say, "I really felt something out there. I had an experience." *Acting is doing.*

‹ GETTING LAUGHS ›

COMEDY IS SERIOUS BUSINESS. When Mike Nichols was directing *Spamalot*, the actors worked out all kinds of funny bits and showed them to him. He laughed and said, "Great, now make me believe it."

Playing comedy is hard. But actors shouldn't be afraid of comedy; it is just another part of the human experience. Many actors think, "This play is a riot. It is one of the funniest plays I have ever read. The audience will be rolling out of their seats." Actors work hard in rehearsal to *punch up* everything that they think is going to get them the laughs they expect. I've know actors who made lists of the places they thought should get laughs.

Come opening night, if the audience doesn't laugh, the play is in trouble. Actors end up devastated when the things that they thought would bring down the house instead land like a lead balloon. The next night, the director tells actors to experiment by playing it straight—by going back to their *objectives*, committing to them, and finding truth in their characters. When actors focus on making everything in the play believable, the comedy, as a result, will follow.

Often, instead of trusting the playwright or the audience, actors will try too hard to be funny. Actors should not try to be funny. It rarely works.

Other times, actors will think too hard about getting a laugh and fail. For example, during an interview with Dick Cavett on his popular TV show, the husband and wife team of Alfred Lunt and Lynn Fontanne were discussing a play in which they both appeared that had a long run in New York followed by an extended tour. Alfred was puzzled that a particular moment of comedy didn't land with the audience. "I should have gotten a laugh when I picked up the tea cup, and I never did," he said. "To this day I don't know why."

Lynn replied, "You didn't get the laugh because you were thinking about getting the laugh."

In situations such as this, actors can't tell the audience when to laugh. But actors, via how an audience reacts, can discover the humor within a play. When playing comedy, actors need to be aware of the audience and work with them. When an audience laughs, actors should hold until the laughs start to fade before delivering their next line. Timing is crucial in comedy. It is something that actors learn from experience and from working with an audience.

Double takes—when we observe or hear something or someone, look away, and then quickly look back to double check what we thought we saw or heard—are effective comedy tools. In the course of our daily lives, we do them all the time. Actors need to be aware of their everyday behaviors, which are often funny. When telling stories to friends, we dramatize events and characters—and are aware of timing. If our friends laugh, then we wait for them to stop before continuing the story.

There are other times when we are not aware of the humor of a situation until after the fact. Arguments are serious and dramatic, but looking back upon them from a distance after time has passed, they often seem silly and make us laugh.

Many times, actors receive big laughs when they play comedy with innocence and simplicity, thus allowing the audience to identify with the humanity of the characters. The audience, in essence, is laughing at themselves.

I learned this firsthand while working on my first performance project at the HB Studio. Ms. Hagen was directing a program that consisted of scenes from J.D. Salinger's short stories and his novel *The Catcher in the Rye*. Several different actors played Holden Caulfield in various scenes from the book. I played Holden while he was on a date at the Rockefeller Center ice skating rink.

In the scene my date and I sat at a restaurant table, drinking soda and looking out on the rink. During rehearsal, we worked with a table, chairs, napkins, and glasses of water with straws. But for the first performance, we were given glasses with real soda and ice, which was new to us. I found myself escaping the frivolities of my date's discussion about college life by playing with the straw in the soda and ice. The audience laughed.

After the scene, Ms. Hagen congratulated us. I told her that I didn't think the scene was funny. She replied, "You made the audience laugh at themselves. They have all been in your shoes."

It is a joyous experience when actors receive laughs. There is nothing quite like an audience's approval in the form of laughter. But some laughs come harder than others. In the final scene of *Tuesdays with Morrie*, the audience cries as Morrie is dying. Then, when Morrie makes jokes about his imminent death, the audience laughs through their tears. For actors, this type of emotional response from an audience represents the ultimate experience.

◄ When Things Go Wrong ►

ACTING IN A PLAY in front of a live audience sometimes feels like walking on a tightrope high in the air without a net below to catch you if you fall. Everyone involved in the production has worked hard to assure that a near perfect package is presented to the audience. The actors, director, designers, and crew attempt to control as much as possible in order to ensure a safe and flawless performance.

Unfortunately, there are times when things somehow manage to go wrong: an actor misses an entrance or forgets their lines, props malfunction or are misplaced, lighting and/or sound problems occur, costumes experience issues, set changes don't work, an actor is injured or gets sick on stage, etc. These troubles seem to occur more often when an audience is present—often on opening night— than they do in rehearsals. Every actor has horror stories of when things have gone wrong.

I have experienced every one of the problems mentioned above— and probably more. When things go wrong, how should actors handle it? What should they do about it? There is no one answer. It is important for actors to keep a level head and concentrate on what can be done to work around the problem(s), such as improvising or going with the flow.

If an actor misses an entrance, it leaves other actors on stage with nothing to do. As a result, they are forced to improvise physical and verbal *actions* while waiting what seems like an eternity for the missing actor to enter. Then, when the tardy character finally arrives, that actor must improvise an apology, explaining why they were late. Everyone scrambles to cover up the faux pas, hoping that the audience won't notice.

Sometimes it is necessary to stop the performance and fix the problem. For example, I once saw a production where an actor fell and cut himself. He was bleeding profusely. The audience lost focus in the play, and their concern shifted to the bleeding actor. That performance should have been stopped by the stage manager and medical attention provided to the actor. Then, the performance could have resumed.

In situations where things go wrong, actors can only do the best that they can. Knowing how to concentrate—and on what to concentrate—is an actor's best bet in any of these unfortunate situations.

◄ After the Performance ►

When the performance is over, actors should forget about it, go out with their colleagues and friends, and share a laugh over a drink or two. It is important that actors do not take their characters home. Actors should step away from the play for a moment. If there is a performance the next day, then when morning arrives, repeat the procedure I outlined at the beginning of this chapter.

◄ Audiences (or the Lack Thereof) ►

In Tom Stoppard's play *Rosencrantz and Guildenstern Are Dead*, the character of The Player confronts Rosencrantz and Guildenstern regarding his theatre company's unattended performance:

> You don't understand the humiliation of it—to be tricked out of the single assumption which makes our existence viable— that somebody is watching ... We ransomed our dignity to the clouds, and the uncomprehending birds listened ... We're actors ... We pledged our identities ... that someone would be watching ... No one came forward. No one shouted at us. The silence was unbreakable, it imposed itself on us; it was obscene.

I don't know the exact number of performances that I have either acted in or directed to a gathering of only a few audience members, but it has been many. The embarrassing "silence" of an empty house was felt by both the actors and the audience. I remember looking out the window, hoping to see audience members arriving late and straggling up the street. But usually the street was empty or people were headed to other destinations.

In the *New York Times,* Mary-Louise Parker spoke of playwright Lanford Wilson:

> Joe Cino's tiny Off Off Broadway room gave birth to great theater on an eight-by-eight stage, some nights for whatever meager audience it could gather. One evening a storm waylaid anyone from attending, and there was not one soul in a seat. The actors all stood there in silence, wondering if they should shuffle out and go home, until Joe said, "Do it for the room." That became the mantra for Joe, and the lucky actors who performed there for no reason other than the joy of it.

That joy is what has driven me as an actor, teacher, and director for over sixty years. It is the same joy I first experienced at age eleven when Aunt Gertrude and I second acted *Angel Street* at the Clinton Playhouse. I have held on to that joy for a lifetime.

Yes, learning the craft of acting has been difficult and coping with rejection has been frustrating. But my almost compulsive need—not for fame, money, or power but to communicate the stories of our collective experiences to an audience—has fueled my journey. This pursuit of becoming a player has been my life's work.

~

ACKNOWLEDGMENTS

I WOULD LIKE TO thank the following people for their assistance in bringing this book to life or for generously contributing in different ways toward my development as an artist.

Atif Rome, my life partner and best friend for over thirty years, who offered many positive suggestions during his early reads of this work. Thank you Atif for your love and support and all your hard work in construction of the studio.

Peter Alan Nichols, my son, for his insight, understanding, and support.

Kathleen Warfel, for reading my first draft of this book and providing encouragement and many illuminating suggestions.

Mark Gardiner, for his editing suggestions and entrusting me with his play *Jesus on Toast*. Thanks for helping with the floods.

j.d.tulloch, for his impeccable editing and knowledge of the English language—and 39 West Press for publication.

Mary Pinizzotto, for her help, encouragement, honesty, and energy. Kudos to her KC Fringe Fest best actress nod for her work on *Jesus on Toast*.

All of my students over the years that have helped me refine the work, especially my long term students: Nancy Marcy, who first put the bug in my ear about writing a book; Kathy Murphy, for her generous contributions to the studio and support of my work; Ellen Loschke, for her organizing work at the studio and helping me pull it together after our floods; Jeannie Blau, who started studying with me at the beginning of the studio, had to stop acting, and is now back in class and wowing audiences all over again.

Dr. Patricia McIlrath (Dr. Mac), Missouri Repertory Theatre Artistic Director, who took a chance and hired me at a critical turning point in my life.

Art Ellison, senior member of Missouri Repertory Theatre, whose helpfulness, kindness, and generosity will never be forgotten.

Joey Kenig, for his beautiful soul, lifetime friendship, great memory, and fabulous proofreading.

Joanna, my wife and creative partner for over twenty years.

All the actors and directors that I have worked with over the years. Each has challenged me, and I feel I have grown as an artist and person as a result of those challenges.

The following people for employing me as an actor, teacher, or director: George Keathly (Missouri Repertory Theatre); Cynthia Levin (Unicorn Theatre); Paul Huff and Lilly Zarda (American Heartland Theatre); Richard Crothers, Dennis Hennessy, and Joe Fox (New Theatre Restaurant); Bob and Karen Paisley (Metropolitan Ensemble Theatre); Jan Sheerin, David McTeer, and Susan Proctor (Rockhurst University); Jim Cox (Park University); Beate Pettigrew (Johnson County Community College); Jeff Church (The Coterie); Herman Johansen (2011 KC Fringe Fest); George Harter (Musical Theater Heritage); Joyce Slater and Glendora Davis (Potluck Productions).

And Dr. Bruce Schwartz, who has kept me alive during my ongoing battle with COPD.

LIST OF EXERCISES

~

LIST OF EVALUATIONS

~

INDEX

~

ABOUT THE AUTHOR

RICHARD ALAN NICHOLS is an actor, teacher, and director. He studied acting as a scholarship student for five years with Uta Hagen at the HB Studio in New York and has taught acting at Washington University, Park University, Avila University, and Rockhurst University. In 1985 he created his own studio, The Actor's Craft Studio, where he instructs beginning, intermediate, and advanced actors.

Nichols' stage credits include: Nonno in The *Night of the Iguana* (Metropolitan Ensemble Theatre), the title role in *The Giver* (The Coterie), Moris in *Permanent Collection* (Unicorn Theatre), Morrie in *Tuesdays with Morrie* (American Heartland Theatre), Harry in *The Sum of Us* (Actors & Artists Against AIDS), Dorn in *The Seagull* (Missouri Repertory Theatre), and many more. His film credits include: James Ivory's *Mr. and Mrs. Bridge*, Steven Soderbergh's *King of the Hill*, and the TV movie *They've Taken Our Children*.

Nichols has directed *Jesus on Toast* (KC Fringe Festival), *You Can't Take It With You* (Rockhurst University), *Anna in the Tropics* (Johnson County CC), *Reckless* (Unicorn Theatre), *The Woolgatherer* (Park University), and many more. He is the author of two plays: *Land* and *Detours*.

Nichols resides with his partner, set and costume designer Atif Rome, in Kansas City, Missouri.

CPSIA information can be obtained
at www.ICGtesting.com
Printed in the USA
BVHW032335210621
609993BV00009B/369/J